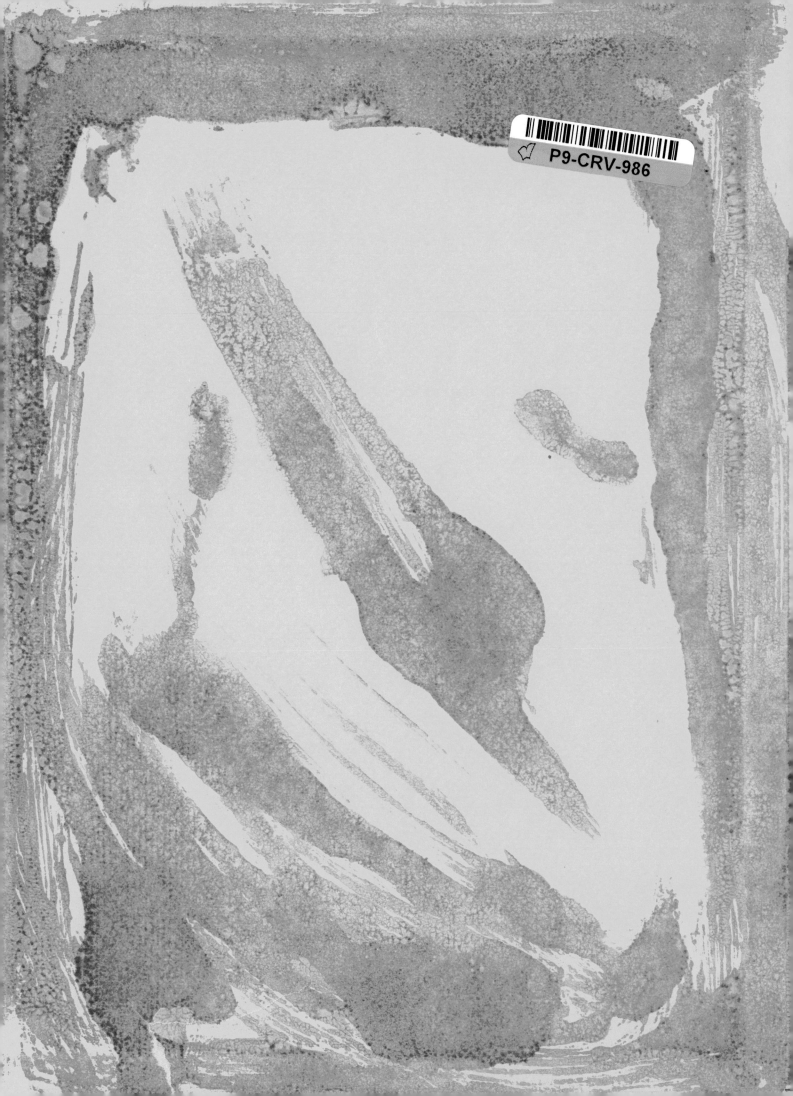

DATE DUE

APR 1 5 1985			
GAYLORD			PRINTED IN U.S.A.

Fonteyn
and
Nureyev

The story of a partnership

Alexander Bland

Times
BOOKS

Acknowledgements

Of course the biggest debt of gratitude for help in preparing this book is due to the subjects of it. The readiness of Dame Margot Fonteyn and Rudolf Nureyev to spare the time to examine the hundreds of photographs submitted to them was matched only by the severity with which they judged them. Special thanks for special assistance are also due to, among others, Miss Neil Ambrose, Miss Myra Armstrong, Miss Suzanne Fleischmann, Mr Keith Money, Miss Bonnie Prandato, Miss Nancy Sifton, Miss Arks Smith, Miss Anna Toumaniantz and Mr Robin Wright. The book owes much to the devoted and expert editing of Miss Tristram Holland and the layout skill of Miss Zena Flax, and to the cooperation of the many photographers who took part in the search for illustrations. Any mistakes in, or omissions from, the attempt to trace the vertiginous orbits of the two stars are entirely my responsibility. AB

The critics quoted are as follows:
Arts Jacques Bourgeois; *Bath Weekly Chronicle* John White; *Daily Express* Noel Goodwin, David Lewin; *Daily Herald* Elizabeth Frank; *Daily Mail* Oleg Kerensky, David Gillard; *Daily Telegraph* Arthur Franks, A. V. Coton; *Daily Worker* Jennifer King; *Dance and Dancers* Peter Williams, John Percival, Clive Barnes, Kate Cunningham; *Dance News* Mary Clarke; *Dancing Times* Mary Clarke, Lelia Moss, James Monahan, Oleg Kerensky; *Die Bühne* Wolfgang Schimming; *Evening News* Duncan Harrison; *Evening Press* Walter Terry; *Evening Standard* Annabel Farjeon, Sarah Jefferson; *Financial Times* Andrew Porter, Clement Crisp, Ronald Crichton; *France-Soir* Jean Cotte; *Glasgow Herald* Edward Mason; *Herald Tribune* Walter Terry; *John O'London's* Caryl Brahms; *La Vanguardia Española* Xavier Montsalvatge; *Le Figaro* Claude Baignères; *Le Monde* Olivier Merlin; *New Statesman* Annabel Farjeon, Ronald Bryden; *New York Daily News* Bill Zakriesen; *New York Journal* Miles Kastendieck; *New York Magazine* Alan Rich; *New York Post* Frances Herridge; *New York Times* Allen Hughes, Clive Barnes, Gay Talese, Anna Kisselgoff; *New Yorker* Winthrop Sargeant; *Scotsman* 'B.C.'; *Spectator* Clive Barnes, Clement Crisp; *Sunday Telegraph* Susan Lester, Edward Mason, Nicholas Dromgoole; *The Guardian* James Kennedy; *The Listener* Oleg Kerensky; *The New Daily* John Percival; *The Observer* Alexander Bland, Peter Brook, Eve Anrep; *The Stage* Eric Johns; *The Sunday Times* Richard Buckle; *The Times* Clive Barnes, John Percival; *The Westminster News* Anthony Gerrard; *Turin Musical Chronicle* Freda Pitt; *Vienna Arbeiterzeitung* Hans Hahnl; *Vienna Kronenzeitung* Hedi Schulz; *Washington Post* Alan Kriegsman.

Frontispiece: Photo of *Marguerite and Armand* by Zoë Dominic

Published by TIMES BOOKS, a division of
Quadrangle/The New York Times Book Co., Inc.
3 Park Avenue, New York, N.Y. 10016
Published simultaneously in Canada by
Fitzhenry & Whiteside Ltd., Toronto.

First published by Orbis Publishing Limited, London 1979

Library of Congress Cataloging in Publication Data
Bland, Alexander
   Fonteyn and Nureyev: the story of a partnership.
   1. Fonteyn, Margot, Dame 1919–   2. Nureyev, Rudolf Hametovitch, 1938–
   3. Dancers – Biography.   4. Ballet.   I. Title
GV1785.A1B57   792.8'092'2 (B)   79-64452
ISBN 0-8129-0860-0
Printed in England by Westerham Press

The growth of a legend

Prelude

Partnering in dance is a form of pair-bonding like marriage (though somewhat more ephemeral). Like marriage, it is a complicated activity with many openings onto failure and many different paths to success. There is no single recipe, no formula for perfection. But sometimes such a notably well-working example appears that it takes on the form of an ideal. Lincoln Kirstein, the famous American writer and dance patron, has inimitably described the result, if not the causes, of such a blessed combination. 'Dancers who, from habit or preference, have frequently danced together come to have a sense of each other's physical presence which, translated into terms of dancing, is revealed to an audience as an exquisite mutual awareness or superhuman courtesy.'

Such close artistic couplings are extremely rare in dance. In the past there have been few names which link themselves automatically together. Vestris and Taglioni seem to hang in history as lone stars. Pavlova and Nijinsky, though they did dance together, were never really a pair (his regular partner was Karsavina). Cerrito had her Saint-Léon, Grisi her Jules Perrot; in our own time Markova and Dolin made a formidable joint attraction. But there has probably never been a conjunction of two dancers which has proved so harmonious, so satisfying, so fruitful and hence so famous as that between Margot Fonteyn and Rudolf Nureyev.

Their presence together on the dance scene was immediately electrifying and lastingly dominant. After their very first performance together in London *The Sunday Times* proclaimed their partnership as 'made in heaven'. Two years later the *Herald Tribune* wrote from New York 'The audience screamed and screamed for half an hour. They were in the presence of greatness and they knew it.' The *New York Times* described the partnership as 'a confluence of dancers where the chemistry, the times and most of all the artistry, all were right. To see Fonteyn was one thing.

Beverley Gallegos

A message from the gallery at the end of a season

To see Nureyev was another thing. But to see Fonteyn and Nureyev together, on the same stage, with their particular love and assurance, was almost indescribably special.'

The extraordinary magic of their performances seemed to be effective on all kinds of audience of many nationalities, though naturally emphasis would be laid on one or other of the partners according to local taste – on the whole British and American audiences seem to have been especially struck by Fonteyn's poise and unforced command of her art, while the public on the European continent responded most quickly to Nureyev's dynamism and drama. But everyone agreed on the uncanny harmony between the two which made a separate judgement on either individual almost meaningless. When the curtain fell audiences would sit as though stunned by some holy fall-out.

The reverberations of their art could be felt far outside the world of ballet. Their appearance together at an airport or a restaurant brought a flurry of cameras into action and their lightest allusion to each other made headlines. Inevitably attempts were made to drum up a romantic attachment between them; but Nureyev laughed it off and Fonteyn would point out that she was, and remained, happily married. Something more elusive, a more indefinable intimacy was afoot, a feeling which could be felt in the theatre by any sensitive viewer. 'When Fonteyn curtseyed before the curtain it might have been Duse,' wrote the drama director Peter Brook after the première of *Marguerite and Armand*, the first ballet written for them. 'And when she and Nureyev stood together, tired and tender, a truly moving quality was experienced; they manifested to that audience a relationship graver, paler and less flesh-bound than those of everyday life.' This was indeed Kirstein's superhuman courtesy.

This book is intended to be a tribute to and to some extent a record of this elusive phenomenon. The account of its development can only be partial – a complete account of the activities of the pair would require an international research team to compile and a volume to set down. The narrative serves only as a kind of temporal skeleton supporting an incredibly rich and varied succession of performances in many parts of the world.

In the same way, efforts to analyse what is essentially an immaterial and inscrutable effect can only scratch the surface of truth. Like scientists trying to isolate the heart of the material universe, we must judge the nature of the forces at work by their effects. These effects have taken the form of ballet, that combination of dance and drama which the two artists have used as their instrument of expression.

In my accounts of the twenty-six dance-pieces – varying from full-length classics to brief duets, which they have performed together, I have made use of quotations from articles written by many critics (including myself) who were present at their performances – where possible at the first performances when impressions were most vivid. This is because the view of a single writer seems to me less illuminating than a chorus of mixed voices – what in art terms is known as 'the informed consensus of opinion' – and because no careful subsequent reconstruction, no 'recollection in tranquillity', can convey the excitement which is so evident in reactions immediately after the event. Since most of the premières took place in London, the majority of the quotations are from London publications (the names of the critics are listed elsewhere). From their descriptions, harmonious but surprisingly varied – though obviously repetitive if they were to be read consecutively – seems to rise an impression of the particular spell cast by the pair.

For later performances, countless comments could be quoted from all over the world. From these it is possible to guess how the two dancers developed their roles after their first try-outs in front of an audience. One surprising discovery is that there was an initial coolness towards their first appearance in some ballets in which they later had great success, and vice versa; there were, for instance, reservations in London about their first *Swan Lake*, while *Paradise Lost* received on the whole wide praise. The ballets in which they have had their greatest success seem to have been, besides the short custom-built *Marguerite and Armand* which became their 'signature ballet', *Giselle, Romeo and Juliet* and, after a controversial start, *Swan Lake*.

By a stroke of fortune several of their performances together have been recorded, either on television or on film. But the still photograph – especially when taken during an actual stage performance – often remains the most eloquent witness. The illustrations in this book have been drawn from many different sources over the whole duration of the partnership so far. They have all been chosen by the dancers themselves from a selection submitted by me.

Below: a scene from *Amazon Forest* – thirteen years after the first appearance of the two dancers together

Mira

Central Press

The partners

The affinity between Fonteyn and Nureyev was evident from the start, but it was as curious as it was unexpected. The two participants were born nearly twenty years and thousands of miles apart into totally different, indeed hostile, cultures. They were opposed physically, one English with a strong streak of Latin, the other Russian but a Tartar by race. They spoke different languages. Their social origins and early beginnings were contrasted. Following the paths across time and space which were to bring them together is like tracking two points of light drawing irrevocably nearer across the darkness, one describing a smooth and steady curve, the other darting forward in a series of violent impulses.

Margot Fonteyn (real name Margaret Hookham) was born in Reigate, a small town in the south of England, in 1919. Her mother was half Brazilian – which may account for her very un-English, slightly oriental, beauty. Like many other middle-class little girls, she was sent to local dancing classes to improve her deportment, starting at the age of four in an academy in a London suburb. Soon she had progressed to ballet classes and passed an exam 'with honours', and her mother quickly realized that she had a daughter with a gift for dancing. When the family moved temporarily to Hong Kong and Shanghai, where her father had been transferred on business, she was sent to take ballet classes with one of the White Russian teachers who had fled eastwards after the Revolution, George Goncharov, an experienced dancer from the Bolshoi. She even appeared in public: 'Miss Peggy Hookham was easily the hit of the performance,' recorded a Tientsin paper. She was eleven, and her course had been set.

Mrs Hookham was now sure of the direction it should take, and on the return of the family to Britain, she sent her daughter to study in London with one of the most famous teachers working there, an ex-Maryinsky ballerina, Serafina Astafieva. Miss Hookham was fourteen and already a well grounded pupil with a determination to go to the top. On being shown a photograph of Pavlova and told that she was 'the greatest dancer in the world', she had replied firmly 'Then I will be the second greatest.'

Mrs Hookham was equally determined. Ninette de Valois had recently opened a school attached to her new Sadler's Wells Ballet company and, realizing that this was the anteroom to a professional career, Mrs Hookham transferred her daughter there. About a week later de Valois herself came to watch a class. 'Who is the little Chinese girl in the corner?' she asked. The teacher explained that, though lately from Shanghai, she was not Chinese. De Valois took her in hand. Soon afterwards Miss Hookham made her real stage debut, as the third snowflake on the left in *The Nutcracker*. The long trajectory to stardom had started.

She was fifteen, a small, dark, impish-looking girl with a soft, easy movement which quickly took her into principal roles. Within a year she was dancing Odette in *Swan Lake* (with an older girl taking the virtuoso part of Odile). It was clear that, barring accidents, time would carry her to the top rank of de Valois' new little company. Now chance intervened – one of those happy eventualities which marked her as the possessor of a

Zoë Dominic

Above: Fonteyn (in attitude) in rehearsal

Right: trying on a costume for *Marguerite and Armand*

Keith Money

Left: an arabesque in the rehearsal room

Right: signing autographs at the stage door at Covent Garden

Leslie Spatt

quality essential to any star, good fortune. The leading dancer of the company, Alicia Markova, decided to leave it to lead an independent troupe of her own (with Anton Dolin). De Valois made a characteristically bold decision. Rather than import a foreign star, she decided to stake everything on her own youthful beginner. Fonteyn became, at seventeen, the principal ballerina of the British national ballet company.

Her career consequently accelerated immediately. At seventeen she danced *Giselle*, at eighteen *Swan Lake*, at nineteen *The Sleeping Beauty*. Experience began to be added to her natural talent under the ever-watchful eye of de Valois. And an equally important gift was laid at her feet: the company included a young choreographer of huge promise who was especially adroit in drawing out the individual gifts of a dancer and in fitting his creations to them. Frederick Ashton was to become almost a co-operator in Fonteyn's development, devising role after role to take advantage of her style and personality. More than that, the whole dancing accent of the company began to take on her own inflections. In later years it began to appear that, unlike other great stars, Fonteyn had no personal

Lipnitzki-Viollet

Left: after a performance in Paris

Right: ready for work in London

style of her own, only a perfection of 'normality'; this (as was to be evident when she danced with other companies) was the opposite of the truth. She had subtly stamped her own individuality on the whole British school.

The rise in prestige of the British company – overshadowed at first by visiting Russian troupes – and its dramatic, still somewhat inexplicable, explosion into popularity during the war years, carried her more and more into the public eye. She floated upwards effortlessly, her ever-stronger technique carrying her safely through the classics, helped by the colourful dramatics of her partner, Robert Helpmann, and her limpid lyricism winning all hearts in the new ballets which Ashton created for her, from *Apparitions* to *Daphnis and Chloë*, from *Cinderella* to *Ondine*. Her combination of personal beauty, talent and feminine charm was irresistible. There can have been few dancers who have been accompanied through their career by such consistent critical acclaim. It was not so much a triumphal march as a long glissade to fame.

The peak of her professional life seemed to have been reached when she led the Sadler's Wells Ballet in *The Sleeping Beauty* on its first visit to New York in 1949. 'Margot Fonteyn is unmistakably a ballerina among ballerinas; last night she conquered another continent,' wrote the critic of the *Herald Tribune*. The whole production was hailed as a triumph, with Fonteyn glittering at its centre, simple, elegant and unruffled. It seemed a climax impossible to repeat let alone surpass.

Her return to Britain was celebrated by the creation of another Ashton role for her, in his *Sylvia*. She suddenly married a Panamanian diplomat,

Rex Features

Left: Nureyev off-stage

Right: rehearsing for a romantic ballet, watched by some of his colleagues

Roberto Arias. In 1956 he was appointed ambassador in London and she was created a Dame of the British Empire. The same year the company received a Royal Charter and in 1957 she opened its fifth New York season, again in *The Sleeping Beauty*. Her position seemed so established as to have become almost stationary. But in 1958 her husband abruptly resigned his ambassadorship while Ashton was creating a final full-length role for her in *Ondine*. In 1959 her name sprang into the headlines accused with her husband of revolutionary activities in Panama. A few months later the Royal Ballet changed her status to that of Guest Artist. She was forty, then considered an advanced age for a ballerina. Her regular partner, Michael Somes, retired and some slackening of tension was noticed in her interpretations of the classics. Her interests seemed to be straying from the theatre.

Though she herself denied it, everything pointed towards a smooth, gentle retirement. Perhaps it would be after her first appearance with the Royal Ballet at its acknowledged mother-theatre, the Maryinsky (now Kirov) Theatre in Leningrad. Three nights after her première there, news came from London that a young Kirov dancer had defected in Paris. His name was Nureyev. With typically happy Fonteyn timing he had appeared dead on cue to speed the final phase of her career like a booster rocket.

Rudolf Nureyev had been born (in a train) in 1938 – about three months after Fonteyn's debut in *Swan Lake* at Sadler's Wells, and about 5000 miles

Michael Peto

away. He came from a poor family and was brought up in conditions of extreme wartime hardship in a village near Ufa, a town near the Ural mountains. Far from being conducted to dance and deportment classes as a child, he had to fight his way – as he was to continue to fight all his life – into his career. He used to sneak away secretly, against the wishes of his father, to indulge in the passion for dancing which had possessed him since he was a little boy. He learned the folk-dances of the region and even contrived to take some lessons in the rudiments of ballet from an old teacher in the neighbourhood. These led to permission to attend classes given in the local opera house and eventually to a few appearances on stage. His big chance came when one day, owing to the absence of one of the participants, he was included in a troupe from the opera house chosen to take part in a Bashkir festival in Moscow.

Above: Nureyev in action in the classroom

Right: in a characteristic pose while resting – relaxed but watchful

Frederika Davis

Left: Nureyev watches a rehearsal

Right: practising at the barre

Once in the capital, he knew where he was going. He presented himself for an audition at the Bolshoi school and impressed the teachers enough to be invited to join it. But he declined; he was set on entering the most famous of all Russian ballet schools, the Leningrad academy where Nijinsky and Pavlova and Ulanova had studied. With the money he had received for his performances he bought a one-way ticket to Leningrad, and, after sixteen hours standing in the train, he reached the door in Rossi street of which he had dreamed so long. It was shut for the holidays. But a week later he was being auditioned by one of the Kirov teachers, who accepted him – with reservations. 'Young man,' she told him. 'You will either become a brilliant dancer or a total failure – and most likely you'll be a failure.'

Disaster seemed very possible. He was already seventeen, an age at which most dancers are finishing their training. Moreover, he was an outsider by both background and temperament. He did not share the interests and common experiences of the other pupils who had been brought up in Leningrad, and the obstacles he had already encountered had made him a difficult character who resisted discipline and suggestions from other people. At the age when Fonteyn had been lovingly guided by parents, teachers and choreographers into the niceties of the classical style, Nureyev was furiously battling his lonely way against the artistic and political establishment of his school. Quick-witted, sharp-tongued and non-conformist by nature, he refused to join the regulation organizations and accepted correction grudgingly, instantly becoming the black sheep of the flock.

Fortunately, the most gifted of all the teachers of boys, Alexander Pushkin, won his confidence and love. He invited Nureyev to stay with him instead of sleeping in the small boys' dormitory to which his junior status assigned him and, together with his wife, took the brilliant but refractory boy under his wing. Within three years Nureyev had passed through the whole course to emerge as a prize pupil in the All-Russian students' competition in Moscow. Both the Bolshoi and Kirov companies offered to engage him. He had no hestitation. In 1958 he became a member, with the rank of soloist, of the Kirov Ballet. He was twenty.

His debut was in a full-length ballet, *Laurençia*, dancing with the company's senior ballerina, Natalia Dudinskaya. In the next few years he took the principal roles in most of the classics in the company's repertoire – *Swan Lake, The Sleeping Beauty, Giselle, Don Quixote, La Bayadère*, appearing opposite the leading ballerinas. This sudden explosion into the top rank was enough in itself to give rise to jealousies which he did little to pacify. But he also proved recalcitrant when he was sent out, between the fortnightly performances which were normal for a principal, on arduous tours to the provinces which he thought damaged his main appearances. He was soon at odds with the company management, as he had been with the school authorities. He acquired an enthusiastic following among the audience, but he was dissatisfied with his opportunities. He felt that he was being artistically restricted (he had been forbidden to dance outside Russia after one stormy excursion) and he was out of sympathy with the authoritarian conformism which ruled in the company. Even his dance style was markedly individual.

The climax came in 1961, while the Kirov was appearing in Paris. At the last moment he had been included in the tour in place of the senior male dancer, Konstantin Sergeyev. His effect on the French audience was electrical and he in return was evidently overwhelmed by the sense of freedom and vitality in the West. Fortified by his acclaim, he openly defied the strict company regulations, staying out late and mixing with foreigners. Messages must have flashed between Paris and Leningrad, and when, at the end of the season the company assembled at the airport to fly on to London, where they were to open a few days later, he was taken aside and told that he was to return to Russia. Guessing that this would mean a final and irrevocable closing of the door, he acted with characteristic dash. He walked across to two French policemen standing in the hall, told them he wished to stay in France and demanded their protection. One hour later the company had gone and he was on his way back to Paris on his own. He had committed himself to a career in the West.

Snowdon

Places and performances

Felix Fonteyn

Fonteyn greets Nureyev in her Covent Garden dressing room before his first performance in London

The orbits of the two artists had drawn dramatically nearer but were not yet to cross. Nureyev had never been (and was not to be) one for pauses in his dancing routine, and immediately accepted an engagement to tour for a year with the Grand Ballet du Marquis de Cuevas, learning the hard way the patterns of ballet in the West. He had little time off as the company travelled round France and Italy, but one week he found the opportunity to fly to Copenhagen to meet a dancer he greatly admired, Erik Bruhn, and to take lessons from a famous teacher, Vera Volkova. It was while he was in her flat one day that the telephone rang, and a call came through from London. It was Margot Fonteyn, asking if Volkova thought Nureyev would be right for a gala she was organizing. Volkova had no hesitation. 'He has something of a genius about him; he has the nostrils,' she announced. 'He's here; you can talk to him.' So for the first time Fonteyn and Nureyev found themselves talking to each other. He agreed to come to London to discuss the project.

The visit was to be secret, to avoid the journalists who hounded the defector wherever he went. He was to assume the name of a Polish dancer who had originally been scheduled to appear in the gala, Roman Jasman; there was to be no publicity, apart from a short interview with a newspaper which had offered to pay his fare. 'It is not surprising that he broke with his old masters; he is exceptionally exceptional,' reported the anonymous columnist.

Through a misunderstanding, there had been no car to meet him at the airport. There was a long delay; finally he took a taxi, arriving in his neat black leather jacket to find Fonteyn in full evening dress, ready to go out. 'As he stepped out of the taxi, Nureyev seemed smaller than I had expected . . . he had a funny pinched little face with that curious pallor peculiar to so many dancers from Russia. I noticed the nostrils at once,' wrote Fonteyn later. They talked (his English was very limited) briefly over tea and suddenly he relaxed. 'His smile was generous and captivating. "Oh, thank goodness" I said. "I didn't know Russians laughed."' As they dined together later that night she noticed something else, an occasional flash of steel in his eyes – 'a manifestation of fear', she realized afterwards. Nureyev had no doubts. 'From the first moment I knew I had found a friend. This was the brightest moment in my life since I came to the West.'

Next evening Fonteyn was due to dance *Giselle* at Covent Garden and asked friends to bring him to watch. He sat with them at the back of the theatre, very upright and attentive, missing nothing. It had not lately been one of her best roles and her performance that night was not exceptional, but Nureyev was taking in her line and musicality, the way she used her eyes.

The following day they discussed the gala programme. Nureyev wanted to dance with her and suggested the *Spectre de la Rose* duet. But she was planning to do it with an English dancer, John Gilpin, and anyway thought the difference in their ages would be an impossible barrier. In the end he danced a pas de deux with the American ballerina Rosella Hightower, and a solo specially arranged by Frederick Ashton. It was while watching him rehearse that Fonteyn got his true measure, his mixture of intense application and clowning. 'He was working like a steam engine . . . I thought he would never get through the solo if he put so much effort into each movement. Surely he ought to save himself somewhere? But I hadn't counted on Rudolf's strength. I think it was from that morning that we took to him wholeheartedly.'

Fonteyn's success at the gala was predictable – she already had the Drury Lane audience at her feet. All eyes were on the young Russian, who tore into his specially slanted solo, all leaps and pantherine twists, like a hurricane and had to repeat his spectacular, if somewhat undisciplined, Black Swan solo. Ninette de Valois, Director of the Royal Ballet, made a typically swift and unorthodox decision; she invited him to join her company as permanent guest. Fonteyn for her part changed her mind abruptly after seeing his performance and agreed to dance *Giselle* with him three months later. After their first rehearsal together she telephoned a friend and said 'I was wrong about the gala'.

The sudden excitement engendered by the young stranger resulted in feverish public anticipation of their first appearance together. All three performances sold out instantly and the opening night took on the character of a life-or-death verdict; in two hours a reputation would be either sealed or killed. The hush during the ballet was almost unbroken – hardly a handclap interrupted the dancing until, when the curtain fell, pandemonium broke out.

'As the two stars of the evening came out to take their bow,' wrote a special editorial in the next edition of the London *Dance and Dancers*, 'a roaring was heard from above and was gradually caught up by all those

Overleaf: rehearsing for their first *Giselle* together at Covent Garden

William Chappell explains to Fonteyn his costume design for Nureyev's debut, while Nureyev and Frederick Ashton discuss the score

Michael Peto

There was no immediate follow-up in London but the two launched into another major classic, *Swan Lake*, in the relative discretion of the Nervi Festival with the Royal Ballet touring company. It foreseeably proved a perfect showcase for the romantic feelings which they could evoke and for the pure classic style which they so eloquently illustrated – perhaps their finest roles together. They also danced together in two more performances of *Giselle* and Nureyev made a number of London appearances in May and June with Yvette Chauviré and Sonia Arova; but it was not till November that the pair burst into the headlines again with the première of a short but breathtaking pas de deux which was to prove another of their most celebrated numbers, *Le Corsaire*. This was followed only three nights later by a first performance together in *Les Sylphides*, an interpretation which was perhaps even more remarkable, though it attracted less attention. Fortunately it is recorded on film.

After a few weeks' pause while Nureyev was recovering from a foot injury the new year, 1963, brought them together for the first time at Covent Garden in *Swan Lake*. For a single performance they also appeared together in the ultra-British *Symphonic Variations*. But these interpretations were overshadowed by a more immediately exciting development.

A rehearsal for *Swan Lake* in Paris

Lipnitzki-Viollet

The validity of the partnership having now been visibly confirmed (though both dancers continued to appear with other partners), it seemed obvious that it should be cemented by a ballet especially devised to exploit it. News began to seep out that Frederick Ashton was working on a short piece for them, and in the autumn it was announced that they would be appearing together in a version of the 'Dame aux Camélias' story. Anticipation became intense as the date of the première, 13 December, 1962, grew near. But Nureyev suffered an injury and the first night had to be postponed. To a formidable publicity build-up – there were interviews, photographs, paragraphs and rumours in every medium – the curtain finally rose three months later, on 12 March, 1963, on the short, highly charged drama which was to become the epitome of their collaboration. *Marguerite and Armand* was rapturously received by the public (though there were critical reservations about the choreography). Piteous appeals began to appear in newspaper agony columns begging for seats at any

Rehearsing *Marguerite and Armand* at the Royal Ballet School in London with some of the rest of the cast

Snowdon

Nureyev discusses a point with the choreographer, Frederick Ashton

Zoë Dominic

Cecil Beaton

Cecil Beaton, equally well known as
photographer and designer, devised
the decor and costumes for
Marguerite and Armand. Left: with
his camera and model. This page:
some of the results

Cecil Beaton

Above: a pause during a rehearsal

Right: facing the camera together

price for the two other performances that month, and three more in the autumn proved just as big a sensation. The glamour of the partnership seemed to have reached a peak.

Only a few months later, in May, they were due to make their debut together in New York and inevitably a barrage of publicity attended it: both *Time* and *Newsweek* devoted their cover stories to Nureyev. But he was still, as he was to remain, only a Guest Artist of the Royal Ballet and the honours of the opening performance (in *The Sleeping Beauty*) went to the home-bred pair, Fonteyn and David Blair. Casts were not advertised in advance and Nureyev appeared opposite Fonteyn only in the second performances of *Giselle* and *Swan Lake* – an arrangement which drew protests from some of the audience. 'Countless enquiries are coming to this office regarding the Royal Ballet's performances,' wrote Allen Hughes in the *New York Times* on 24 April, a few days before the opening night. 'And the question is always the same – on which days will Margot Fonteyn and Rudolf Nureyev appear?'

The verdict on their eventual debut was almost unanimous. 'There can be no argument that Dame Margot has danced more beautifully than ever before,' Walter Terry was writing in the *Herald Tribune* on 5 May. 'The youthful Nureyev, almost twenty years her junior, has given her new theatrical inspiration. Combine the smoulder, the mystery, the dynamic presence, the great streaks of vivid movement which Nureyev gives us with the beauty, the radiance, the womanliness, the queenliness and the shining movements of Dame Margot, and the cheers that have shaken the old Met to its foundations are explained . . . This, rightly or wrongly, was the Royal Ballet; this, while Fonteyn and Nureyev were representing the most ephemeral, the most fleeting of all the arts, was ballet itself.'

The success of the partnership in London had been repeated even more strongly (it was hailed also immediately afterwards in Canada). But its sensational nature brought almost immediate repercussions. In London one critic had voiced, after their first triumph, apprehensions that the sudden invasion of the young Russian might crack the seamless integrity and unanimity of the Royal Ballet. Fears were expressed in circles close to the management that Fonteyn herself might be seduced away from loyalty to the style and needs of the company of which she had become the prime embodiment. It was not long before an American added his misgivings. On 11 May the regular critic of the weekly *Saturday Review* had warmly praised the achievement of the two. 'He is a brilliantly sympathetic partner with the strength to make his lifts easily and decisively and the power to sustain them in any attitude required. Little wonder, then, that Fonteyn danced her way through both ballets with a zest and enthusiasm that added immeasurably to all the artistry traditionally hers.' But in the next issue a different voice spoke, or rather boomed. John Martin, the seventy-year-old doyen of American dance critics – he had retired from the *New York Times* only the previous year after a thirty-five-year career – contributed a whole article devoted to castigating Nureyev and his collaboration with Fonteyn. 'It was a black day for the Royal Ballet when . . . he arrived in London as a roving cause célèbre and moved in on the company,' he wrote. 'The Prince in *Swan Lake* may well be the most boring figure ever conceived by a choreographer, but Nureyev, unwilling

Jennie Walton

A rehearsal of the Kurdish dance from *Gayane* takes place somewhat incongruously in the Roman theatre in Athens

to let well alone, succeeds in making him actively offensive . . . To see him as Fonteyn's partner is an unhappy experience, whatever the ballet . . . She is, after all, an exquisite part of a legend, and it is difficult not to feel somehow embarrassed; she has gone, as it were, to the grand ball with a gigolo.'

This conservative attitude to Nureyev's new style of partnering, coupled with the ungallant reference to the difference in their ages, produced an explosion of indignation from some of those who disagreed with him on both sides of the Atlantic. Arnold Haskell, the nearest British equivalent to Martin, wrote in the *Dancing Times*: 'After a very long experience of ballet criticism I have never seen anything to equal Mr John Martin's article', and remarked that it 'merely confirms what I have long felt, that Mr Martin has little real understanding of ballet'. Knives were flashing. But in retrospect this cry of anguish from a veteran American champion of the old school can be judged as a tribute to the fresh approach which was to change the whole concept of a dance duet over the next decades.

After New York and an extended tour of Canada the pair went off during the summer months with a small group of Royal Ballet dancers on an extended tour which took them to France, Greece, Israel, Japan, Honolulu and San Francisco. For this they devised an extract from *La Sylphide* which was their first introduction to Bournonville choreography and which was to prove a useful ingredient in subsequent mixed programmes, as well as a pas de deux from *Gayane*. This was followed by a season in Paris leading the Royal Ballet's touring section in *Swan Lake* at the Champs Elysées theatre. It was the turn of the French public to see and salute the magical couple.

Nureyev danced regularly at Covent Garden during the autumn, and at the end of November he was invited to mount his first work on the company – a reproduction of the 'Shades' scene from *La Bayadère*. This example of Petipa at his most purely classical had been part of the programme on the Kirov Ballet's visit to London – Nureyev was to have danced in it himself – and became a fine showcase for the pair and an invaluable contribution to the Royal Ballet repertoire over the next decade. A few days after the première Fonteyn and Nureyev presented their extract from *La Sylphide* to the London public at a Royal Academy of Dancing gala at Drury Lane. Their debut in a new production of *Swan Lake* before Christmas had to be postponed when Nureyev was injured by being knocked down by a scooter.

1964 was to prove an even busier and more productive year. In March they did half a dozen performances at Covent Garden (*Swan Lake* and *Marguerite and Armand*). In April Nureyev created two new roles, in *Images of Love* and a revival of Helpmann's *Hamlet*, before setting off with Fonteyn to Stuttgart, where they danced Cranko's version of *Swan Lake*, and then Australia, to appear with the Australian Ballet in *Swan Lake* (yet another production) and *Giselle*.

Back in England they ran into tragedy. They had promised to appear in June in the Bath Festival at a special performance with the Western Theatre Ballet. Kenneth MacMillan had written a short duet for them, *Divertimento*, to Bartók's Sonata for solo violin, which was to be played

Working out the movements for Kenneth MacMillan's *Divertimento*, watched by the choreographer

Keith Money

Keith Money

Zoë Dominic

Left: an elegant rehearsal pose

Above: shooting a scene from the film of MacMillan's *Romeo and Juliet* at Pinewood Studios. It was directed by Paul Czinner

by Yehudi Menuhin, director of the Festival, and they would do their *La Sylphide* excerpt. The night before the opening, Fonteyn got a telephone call from Panama telling her that her husband had been wounded in a shooting incident. She duly performed her two duets with Nureyev – the new *Divertimento* was encored – before flying off to Panama, where she found that the injuries were worse than she had thought; a high degree of paralysis (which proved permanent) had resulted.

During the summer Nureyev was back in London rehearsing his production of the full-length ballet *Raymonda* for the Spoleto Festival in Italy. In June the final touches were being added in the little theatre at Spoleto when, just before the final rehearsal, Fonteyn was told that her husband had had a relapse. She had to leave immediately (fortunately it was a false alarm) and returned only for the last performance. The Royal Ballet touring company, on whom the production had been mounted, then moved on to Lebanon, where, before the impressive ruins at Baalbek, Fonteyn and Nureyev again danced *Raymonda*, as well as *The Sleeping Beauty* pas de deux and, a new venture together, Helpmann's nightmare vision of *Hamlet*.

After the briefest of holidays the two were in Vienna again where they appeared in October in the new version of *Swan Lake* which the indefatigable Nureyev had mounted – an occasion marked by the issue of a commemorative postage stamp by the Austrian authorities. Back in London after this strenuous enterprise, the two were soon at Covent Garden again for a whole series of performances, interrupted by a new work arranged by Nureyev for the Royal Academy of Dancing gala, a revival of the old *Paquita* grand pas by Petipa.

1965 was to see another major vehicle for the pair, MacMillan's *Romeo and Juliet*, to the Prokoviev score. This was born in February – in the middle of a busy schedule of appearances at Covent Garden, during which

Snowdon

they found time to fly to Washington to dance *Le Corsaire* at a gala to celebrate the presidential inauguration of Lyndon Johnson – and proved a winner from the start. Though only one of a team of partners to interpret the roles (originally intended for Lynn Seymour and Christopher Gable), they stamped their image indelibly on the ballet, and starred in the film which was quickly made of it.

In April Fonteyn sustained a sprain while rehearsing but was able to lead the company to New York in the summer – its eighth American tour, this time featuring the new *Romeo and Juliet*. The work proved as successful in New York as it had been in London. 'Although Mr Nureyev and Dame Margot were in the spotlight nearly throughout, it was not really a star attraction but rather a production that focused on the whole company . . . When the curtain fell there were 30 curtains calls. It took 36 minutes for the applause to stop . . . They continued to shout from the orchestra and the boxes above: Nureyev! Margot! Nureyev! Margot!' wrote the *New York Times*. The two stars were seen as leaders of a great company, not outside it.

Above: off-duty in Vienna

Right: arriving to perform at the White House in Washington

Travel is an important element in the lives of both dancers

Judy Cameron

Left: an airport portrait

The autumn saw them together again in *Raymonda*, but this time in a revised and redesigned version, and dancing with the Australian Ballet. They opened in Birmingham in November, and toured several cities in Europe with the company, including Paris. Finally it reached London, where its première (at the New Victoria Theatre) was turned into a gala performance for the Royal Academy of Dancing – the last of a memorable series.

The next year, 1966, was to present no new openings for them, though they danced together at Covent Garden on an average about once a week in the first half of the year. Nureyev was busy with new productions elsewhere (*Tancredi* in Vienna in May, *The Sleeping Beauty* in Milan in September – a production in which Fonteyn was to dance later – and *Don Quixote* in Vienna in December). It was not until Boxing Day that they tackled an important new ballet together – as Aurora and Prince Charming in *The Sleeping Beauty*. This was a ballet in which they had both excelled separately for many years and, after the necessary adjustments, they made it one of their most striking achievements.

During the first months of 1967 they were dancing together regularly at Covent Garden, introducing at a gala in February (Fonteyn–Nureyev premières were apt to become gala occasions almost spontaneously) a short ballet, *Paradise Lost*, by Roland Petit. This uncompromisingly modern work came as something of a shock to many of their faithful supporters; the unromantic mood, pop art designs and angular movements seemed alien to their accepted image. It was not popular and it

Left: a rickshaw at Disneyland in California

Below: self-drive – the most reliable form of transport

44

proved equally unsuccessful in the Royal Ballet's New York season that summer. However, they made headline news in a different way towards the end of the American tour when, during a season in San Francisco, they were invited after the show to a party at a house in the 'hippy' district of the city. Soon after their arrival it was raided by police, after a tip-off about drugs. If the whole thing had been arranged by a publicity agent it could not have been more effective. Photographs of the two stars under arrest appeared all over the world under sensational headlines. The notion of the First Lady of British Ballet in handcuffs seemed unthinkable to readers unfamiliar with her adventurous spirit and even the shock-haired Tartar seemed an improbable subject for drug addiction. The Director of the Royal Opera House appeared on television in a dinner jacket to declare that he knew for a fact that they were both non-smokers. Bailed out for $300 each, they were discharged in the small hours of the morning without a stain on their characters.

On their return to Europe they danced together in Paris, in *Paradise Lost* (Petit was Director of the Opéra Ballet at the time) and also in Sweden where Nureyev was preparing another new production, *The Nutcracker*.

Left: burning up surplus dance-energy in Toronto

Below: both dancers have a special love of swimming, boats and the sea

Associated Press

Felix Fonteyn

A much-publicized incident in which police raided a party attended by the dancers in San Francisco

Syndication International

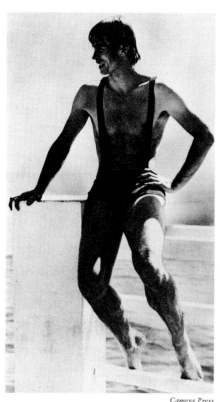

Camera Press

Tickets for the Stockholm performance of *Swan Lake* reached a record black market price of over £100 each.

Fonteyn did not appear at Covent Garden during January 1968, but Nureyev embarked on a small new role in Ashton's *Jazz Calendar* during the month. Fonteyn joined him there in February for a few performances (*Giselle*, *Swan Lake* and *Romeo and Juliet*) before he launched his new *Nutcracker*; this demands that the ballerina should impersonate in the first scenes a girl of nursery age, a part which Fonteyn probably felt she had outgrown. They came together for two or three performances (*Les Sylphides*, *Marguerite and Armand* and *Swan Lake*) before appearing in a work new to them, Ashton's *Birthday Offering*, in which they danced the central pas de deux. The summer found them together again in New York with the Royal Ballet, performing works which were by now established favourites. Afterwards they toured with the smaller company round Europe, introducing audiences in Holland, Switzerland, Germany,

France, Monaco, Italy, Spain and Portugal to their partnership. In October they flew to Iran to appear in a gala celebrating the Shah's birthday.

It was now almost seven years since they first danced together. That spring they performed at Covent Garden as frequently as ever before, finishing at the end of March with the première of another ballet by Roland Petit, *Pelléas et Mélisande*. Though less modern in style – and distinctly more romantic – than *Paradise Lost*, this was even less successful and survived only a few performances. In April they set off for another season at the Met in New York, a six-week spell followed by a Canadian tour – over three months in all. Somehow they managed to live up to the inordinate expectations which by now attached to their every appearance. After their opening in *Swan Lake* the *New York Times* wrote: 'Both know – having triumphed over so many laudatory press notices erecting their

Above: Roland Petit, the French choreographer, dines with his wife Zizi Jeanmaire, Nureyev and Fonteyn

Right: a rehearsal for Petit's *Pelléas et Mélisande*

impossible standards of expectation – their true selves, and can dance
them out with all the honesty of self-knowledge. Together they have the
odd, essentially unbelievable magic of legend made fact.' On arrival back
home in the autumn, they appeared in *The Sleeping Beauty*, *Swan Lake*,
Romeo and Juliet and *La Bayadère* – a busy conclusion to a rewarding year
together.

Andrew Karney

They opened at Covent Garden the next year, 1970, with a couple of
performances of *Giselle* and then a piece they had danced in together
abroad but not in London – the newly designed Act III from *Raymonda*.
They performed regularly throughout February, after which Nureyev was
taken up with a new ballet (Rudi van Dantzig's *Ropes of Time*). However,
he joined Fonteyn for the Royal Ballet's twelfth season in New York and
they were together in London throughout June and July, their appearances culminating in a gala marking Frederick Ashton's retirement as
Director of the Royal Ballet, at which they danced for the first time an
extract from one of his earliest ballets, *Apparitions*. The same year
Fonteyn appeared in Milan in Nureyev's own *Sleeping Beauty*, and they
ended the year in London with two performances of *Romeo and Juliet*.

In some ways the following year marked a turning point in the
partnership. Fonteyn had begun to be increasingly active with companies
other than the Royal Ballet, dancing in Germany, South Africa, America
and France and for a long season with the Australian Ballet; while
Nureyev's interests were moving in the direction of more experimental
styles of dancing. In 1971 they performed only eight times together at
Covent Garden (six performances of *Marguerite and Armand* and two of
Swan Lake), though they also appeared together in *The Sleeping Beauty*
with Petit in Marseilles.

There were no new roles for the pair in 1972. John Cranko wrote a new
ballet for Fonteyn, *Poème de l'Extase*, while Nureyev had a new role in
Jerome Robbins' *Afternoon of a Faun*, but, though they performed
together frequently both at Covent Garden and during the annual season
in New York, they stuck mainly to *Swan Lake*, *The Sleeping Beauty*,
Romeo and Juliet and *Marguerite and Armand*. The next year, 1973, was
again a lean one for Fonteyn–Nureyev admirers. Fonteyn had seemed
slightly off-form in two performances of *Swan Lake* the previous
November, but on 11 January she tried again with Nureyev as her
Siegfried. 'Dame Margot once again established that control of the ballet
that is the prerogative of the great artist,' recorded the *Financial Times*. At
a gala two nights later they danced *Le Corsaire* together; but the rest of the
year saw only seven joint appearances from them.

During all the years they had been dancing together they both continued
to make frequent appearances with other partners (except in *Marguerite
and Armand*), and Nureyev in particular had a busy season at Covent
Garden in 1973. But the rhythm of their joint performances was visibly
slowing down and the next year, 1974, it stopped altogether – for the
simple reason that Fonteyn did not make a single appearance at Covent
Garden that year or the following year, 1975, except to appear with
Nureyev at a gala in March in a pas de deux extracted from John
Neumeier's *Don Juan*. There was a gap of almost exactly two years during
which time they did not appear together in London, though they made a

Rex Features

Andrew Karney

A study in hats – hers, his and one to fit both

Associated Newspapers

bold excursion into modern dance in New York in 1975 when they launched a new ballet by Martha Graham, *Lucifer*, in June, performing it again, with José Limon's *The Moor's Pavane*, in Washington in July.

Then, on 5 January, 1976 they suddenly danced three performances of *Romeo and Juliet* at Covent Garden. Except for brief pas de deux (Ashton arranged two – *Amazon Forest* and *Hamlet Prelude*), these were to be their last appearances together with the Royal Ballet. But London saw them again in the 1977 Nureyev Festival in *Les Sylphides*. And in the 1979 version of the same Festival, only a few weeks after her sixtieth birthday gala which many mistook for a farewell performance, Fonteyn un- expectedly appeared as a nymph who becomes the erotic focus of Nijinsky's *L'Après-midi d'un Faune* – with Nureyev, of course, as the Faune. To cap this surprise, Fonteyn danced the last two performances (that season) of *Le Spectre de la Rose* with Nureyev. The curtain comes down as the ballerina blissfully recalls a magical encounter.

After the curtain falls come the flowers, cheers, clapping, bows and curtsies

Ted Griffiths

The partnership

Clearly the partnership has been an exceptional theatrical event. In retrospect we can see that, in its heyday, it dominated not only the Royal Ballet but the whole spectrum of dance in the Western world (with reverberations spreading outside it). A kind of touchstone of togetherness has been set up, by which other collaborations must be judged. Not unnaturally, both dancers have been questioned repeatedly about the secret of their extraordinary harmony. Both have been hesitant about answering, manifestly because it grew from, and rests on, instinct rather than intellect, chance rather than design, subconscious reactions in place of intellectualizing (though much thinking and discussion was involved). This was a kind of celestial accident. To probe into its components is like trying to analyse a moonbeam: when you turn the torch of enquiry on it there is nothing there.

Yet something can be deduced from looking at its accompanying circumstances. The first noticeable characteristic is that it was a natural happening, neither planned nor even foreseeable. When Fonteyn agreed to the suggestion that she should dance with the unknown young Russian she had no inkling what the consequences would be. If anybody can claim a vision of the future it is Dame Ninette de Valois, Director of the Royal Ballet, who casually proposed the experiment. 'De Valois told me that Rudolf would dance *Giselle* at Covent Garden in February, three months ahead,' Fonteyn has recorded, '"Do you want to do it with him?" she asked. My immediate reaction was to say "Oh my goodness. I think it would be like mutton dancing with lamb."' She consulted her husband and they arrived at a hard-headed decision. 'We came to the conclusion that Rudolf was going to be the big sensation of the next year and I had better get on the bandwagon or else get out. I called de Valois to thank her for asking me and accepted.' Nureyev had had no such hesitation. When invited to make his debut at Fonteyn's gala he had agreed on condition that he could dance either with her or with the Soviet ballerina Ulanova. Such presumption by a boy of twenty-two amused her; but she must have been flattered. (In the end he consented to dance with another partner, lured by the promise of a new solo by Ashton.)

The other major feature of their partnership was clear from the start. This was no smooth dovetailing of similarities. On the contrary it was the confrontation of two very positive and contrasting personalities. On the one side was an experienced ballerina of many years standing, idolized already for her own achievements, the loyal figurehead of a solidly established company moulded in many ways round her own gifts. She could rightly claim the authority of a *prima ballerina assoluta*. Serene and regal simplicity was her hallmark, with a charming self-discipline which appeared unshakeable. Her long schooling and careful training gave her dancing a sense of simple distinction as finely observed and unostentatiously carried out as a piece of English tailoring. With her unchallenged authority and her diplomatic status she seemed the essence of well-bred poise.

Her new partner was the opposite in almost every way. Half her age, he

A rehearsal for *Marguerite and Armand*

had been born into a culture remote from the West, let alone Britain. He had forced his way into ballet school and thrust through its training at headlong speed by sheer talent and determination, artistically a dissident who questioned every inch of tradition and custom, and eventually exploded out of his parent company. Impulsive and undisciplined, a rebel whose only cause was his own dancing mission, his ruthless intensity and passion seemed impossible to reconcile with Fonteyn's cool restraint.

Physically they were complementary. Trim, slim and delicate, Fonteyn looked more feminine and vulnerable than ever beside Nureyev's muscular and sinuous frame. Her simple, gentle style was even more noticeable against his highly charged and sometimes baroque theatricality. Her exquisite oval face took on additional beauty beside his wild, high-cheekboned features. The vibrations which the Impressionist painters discovered in the dialectic of what they called 'simultaneous contrast' were

The appearance of spontaneous harmony results partly from detailed discussion and many try-outs

Zoë Dominic

easy to perceive. But would they be resolved in true synthesis? Could the two styles, the two individualities, be blended?

There seem to be several reasons why the answer was, yes. The first and much the most important was an affinity of temperament. Fonteyn's quick intelligence and love of fun found an immediate answer in Nureyev's character. The adventurous streak in her personality, known only to those close to her, responded to his reckless dynamism, while she could professionally appreciate his knowledge, dedication and the relentless pursuit of perfection which made up one side of a character superficially labelled tempestuous. From the first (and the credit for this lies with Fonteyn) they approached their work together as equals. 'With a new partner there is some carpentry necessary to fit the two versions together. . . . Most of them say "I will do it your way, how does it go?" Rudolf said, however, "Don't you think this way is better?" We entered into some negotiations and each altered a few steps here and there. What mattered to me most was the intensity of his involvement in the role.' With the humility of the real artist she accepted technical suggestions. He, on his part, admired equally her dancing and her approach to dancing. 'From the first I found I could work with Margot with complete understanding,' he has said. 'Though she was a great dancer with enormous experience she accepted my attitude as though we were on the same level. But she did not agree with everything – there was no condescension, no English politeness. It was wonderful.'

That this mutual understanding flowed into their performances was because both had the gift of translating emotion into movement – the very basis of their art. To both of them – and perhaps particularly to Nureyev – an intense and sustained interaction between the two partners, independent of the audience, is an absolute necessity to a good performance. 'Dancing with Fonteyn is always exciting . . . there is something to argue with,' he says. Even the most formal pas de deux, the kernel of a whole evening's collaboration, is to these two a continuation of a dialogue, a conversation, not a 'supported solo' in which the man is a mere prop. (That style arose in the nineteenth century based on the domination of the ballerina and the use of the point-shoe. It had not been the practice in earlier times, nor is it in modern dance – you only have to think of Fred Astaire and Ginger Rogers.)

This conception of partnering, in which – as in opera – a duet involves an equal contribution from both, was something new. Sometimes part of the man's role is to show off the ballerina; but Nureyev never became a passive 'porter' in the old manner (one of John Martin's complaints was that he would sometimes hold his arm higher than Fonteyn's in an arabesque), just as Fonteyn never lost touch with him to make an effect with the audience. They seemed aware of each other even when their backs were turned. When their eyes met, a message passed.

This basic personal rapport – for they are both gifted with a warm human presence on stage – expresses itself, as can be seen in photographs, by an extraordinary physical unanimity. Their limbs seem to fall naturally along the same line, their heads to incline instinctively in unison. 'They dance as if their minds were totally at peace,' wrote one critic. In the same way their phrasing and timing of a step or group of steps has always been

Richard Levin

M-A Durrazzo

effortlessly in tune – refuting incidentally those critics who have maintained that Fonteyn is a musical dancer while Nureyev is not. This sustained and unforced harmony gives a freedom and variety which no amount of practice or rehearsal can achieve. Like two experienced actors playing against each other, Fonteyn and Nureyev have always been able to vary their interpretations minutely from evening to evening, evoking instant response to every change.

This does not mean that their performances have not been rehearsed. On the contrary, they have always spent exceptionally long, intense hours discussing and preparing a ballet. For Fonteyn, Nureyev's fresh suggestions came less as an obstacle than as a stimulus. There can seldom have been an established ballerina with such flexibility and the humility and practicality to seize on and turn to advantage what might well have been rejected for reasons of prestige. Besides absorbing technical tips, she used

Rehearsing two scenes from *Marguerite and Armand*; below: the moment of surrender; right: the pain of separation

his inborn audience-appeal and sensational bravura as a hone on which to sharpen her own talent. 'I found the competition with Rudolf really stiff,' she confesses with relish, like a champion proud of rising standards of performance. Nureyev responded instantly to her artistic generosity; and her apparently effortless mastery, quite apart from his sheer enjoyment of sharing in it, made his appearances with her invariably among his best, while her judgement, sensitivity and experience were a continuous help to his interpretations.

The contrast between their styles and temperaments has often been presented as the embodiment of classical cool and romantic fire, as Apollo linked to Dionysus. Though perhaps apt in general, the analysis is far from exact. 'It was paradoxical,' Fonteyn has written, 'that the young boy everyone thought so wild and spontaneous in his dancing cared desperately about technique, whereas I, the cool English ballerina, was so

Snowdon

much more interested in the emotional aspect of the performance.' In the same way observers of Fonteyn might have remembered her occasional fits of sudden obstinacy, her unpredictability, the adventurous streak which relished her husband's political adventures (including a night in jail). Both of them are compounded of opposites; miraculously, they found a way of playing them off against each other, like a series of chords in which no note dominates but the intervals and relationships undergo constant change.

Though they were an equal attraction from the start, their relationships with the public and, even more, with the critics were very different. Fonteyn was already a favourite figure, as much respected as loved – a goddess of feminine virtue, charm and integrity. Nureyev, an acknowledged rebel and loner, became fixed in the public mind as a stormy petrel whose glamour lay partly in his untamed wildness. This was an unusual image for a ballet star, and produced the appropriate love-hate reactions. From the start this 'tiger in need of a haircut' as a New York headline proclaimed him (his unkempt locks – shortish by today's standards – regularly earned him reproaches for untidy dancing) was a

A joke shared during rehearsals

Zoë Dominic

An unconventional manoeuvre which is more difficult than it looks

regular target for critical sniping. It was precisely this marriage between chaste and elegant poise and daredevil unconventionality which made the match so instantly dramatic, a Heathcliff paired with the Lady of Shalott. The image, though effective, was hardly based on fact. When Nureyev swears during a rehearsal – as he often does – Fonteyn is not the one to be shocked or disconcerted. Beneath her unshakeable calm and courtesy, she is basically as tough and resilient as he; which is one reason why he respects her.

The invigorating effect on Fonteyn's dancing occasioned by the arrival of Nureyev has often been remarked, as well as the benefits he derived from performing with such a cool and experienced partner. But the interaction was very complicated. So far as emotion is concerned Nureyev seems only to have released something which was already there and had always been a part of Fonteyn's art – though never before so openly – new depths were revealed, not new areas. After her first triumphant *Sleeping Beauty* in New York in 1949, Lincoln Kirstein wrote to a friend, 'Fonteyn made a very great impression. She is a lovely dancer, but she seems

Below: a pause for refreshment

Right: the two separate figures fuse to
form a double image

Snowdon

Left: Nureyev in his customary leg-warmers

Right: Fonteyn in a practice skirt

Zoë Dominic

Snowdon

Contrasts of mood during rehearsal

Reg Wilson/Camera Press

Discussing technical problems

. . . unawakened. She has a magical pall over her; she seems to breathe through a haze behind which there may be a brilliant presence, but it is not yet brilliantly announced.' With Nureyev the haze dissolved and the star shone out. To quote the *New York Times* in 1967: 'The catalyst of Mr Nureyev has created a new dancer and that new dancer is the greatest dancer in the world.'

A striking change came, too, over the technical side of her dancing. It acquired an attack and brilliance she had never previously displayed. Nureyev brought her some of the secrets of Russian training – in some ways he was more academically demanding than she – but he also brought her something of his own: a willingness to take risks. It was an attitude to which, as her close friends would have expected, she responded instinctively, just as he found new discoveries in her stagecraft and her intelligent and logical approach to every role. The benefits were manifold and two-way.

If to be lucky is an essential qualification of stardom, both dancers vividly displayed their claims (the role of de Valois as the benign figure presiding over the partnership must never be overlooked). For Nureyev the opportunity to work closely with a ballerina of her calibre gave him the chance to develop in a sympathetic and helpful atmosphere. For Fonteyn, a dancer who had reached such eminence that the only way forward seemed to be downwards, the sudden appearance of a partner who would be a rival and an innovator as well as an ever-ready support presented a challenge and an inspiration which drew out qualities which had remained half-hidden. For the public it produced performances which set standards that have changed the course of ballet history.

Looking back over the partnership, its duration seems unexpectedly short. The period during which they hung in the zenith of the ballet sky, dazzling audiences in city after city week after week, lasted no more than twelve years – only a segment out of the careers of both artists. Latterly their appearances together have been more in the nature of rare treats. Even at its height, the total count of their shared performances at Covent Garden never exceeded twenty-five in a year (in 1963, out of a company total of 142) – less than two hundred altogether in seventeen years. It was not the number of their appearances which, as it seemed at the time, tended to obliterate and obstruct other dancers, but their quality. The barrage of publicity and the frenzied demand for tickets for Fonteyn–Nureyev evenings were a mark of recognition that these were occasions which would never recur.

Something exceptional had happened. How do the participants see it? Understandably, they find it easy to feel, impossible to express. 'When I look across the stage I do not see a man I know, talk to every day. I see the character of the ballet, for he is absorbed in his role,' Fonteyn has said of Nureyev. 'It's not her, it's not me, it is the sameness of the goal,' says Nureyev. 'She convinces me.'

Those who saw them together were convinced – and they can count themselves lucky.

Roles and reactions

The ballets in which the two dancers have appeared together are arranged in the following pages in the chronological order of their first performance. Some ballets have been more fully and successfully recorded than others – the best are not always the most photogenic nor the most illuminatingly discussed – and the amount of space devoted to a ballet is not intended to reflect its importance. My aim has been to give an impression of the partnership as a whole.

Giselle

First performance together London, 21 February, 1962
Choreography Jean Coralli/Jules Perrot **Music** Adolphe Adam
Design James Bailey

I T WAS the oldest of all the ballet classics, *Giselle*, which launched the Fonteyn–Nureyev partnership. The simple tale of an innocent girl wronged by a nobleman who, after her death, is redeemed by remorse – a story related in gothic terms of madness, suicide and ghosts – proved a perfect vehicle for the two dancers. Its blend of lyricism, pathos and drama allowed them to deploy their special quality – the translation of classical movement into romantic emotion.

Fonteyn had been dancing *Giselle* since she was nineteen but – at least in recent years – the full dramatic depths of the role seemed to elude her. Nureyev on the other hand, had made Albrecht one of his most successful parts in Russia. His interpretation was different from the normal British one. His detailed acting (labelled by some critics 'Stanislavskian') and expressive dancing presented a feckless, infatuated aristocratic boy encountering real love for the first time. He drew from Fonteyn a vivid response. Suddenly the whole ballet came to life.

'For the Russian emigré, Mr Nureyev, it was a literally remarkable debut', wrote *The Times*. 'For Dame Margot it can be attested that her Giselle had never proved more satisfying.' 'Fonteyn's Giselle may be a familiar joy but this time she excelled herself,' *The Guardian* noted. 'As for Mr Nureyev, it was to be expected that his classical dancing, as such, would be astonishing. And so it proved. What was less to be expected was that his whole interpretation of the role would be so definite and so convincing.' *The Sunday Times*, under the heading 'Perfect Foil for Fonteyn', wrote: 'Fonteyn . . . gave the performance of a lifetime. Her own rapturous dancing was complemented by Nureyev's and also by his sure, subtle partnering . . . We have come to think of ballet partnerships as being made in the classroom and on the stage over the years of patient working together, but on Wednesday we learned that they are made in heaven.'

Arnold Haskell, doyen of British critics, recorded that Nureyev's dancing 'always at the service of the actor', was magnificent, while his partnering and taking of curtain calls 'has the dignity of the true artist. Dame Margot Fonteyn, who had clearly inspired her partner, was in turn inspired by him. It was a truly memorable evening.' The *Evening Standard* agreed. 'As a partner of Fonteyn, Nureyev is beyond compare.'

The Observer observed that '*Giselle* is essentially a long pas de deux, with both roles offering equal dramatic depth . . . The vital importance of each to the other was spelt out for all to see by the sudden gain in Margot Fonteyn's interpretation.' The *Daily Express* found that 'The prima ballerina has not danced such a moving and ecstatic Giselle in a long while. Certain it is . . . that Albrecht can never be the same again.'

The editor of *Dance and Dancers*, after the first three appearances of Fonteyn and Nureyev in the ballet, found them 'some of the most memorable performances in the history of the Royal Ballet. I would like to think also that they herald a new era in which the company reaches even greater heights of hospitality to the world's great dance stars. Nationalism is a fine thing but internationalism should be ballet's ultimate horizon.'

But the new interpretation did not please everybody. The *Financial Times* found it 'an ill-matched partnership – on the one hand a fully worked-out, masterly interpretation, on the other a promising but immature sketch.' This critic was shocked to see the young foreigner performing opposite the top ballerina and not with 'one of the younger dancers'. The *Daily Telegraph* critic agreed and found that 'all tragic quality, all pathos and dignity had been removed from the plot. What we saw was a nicely calculated piece of balletic fireworks in which Mr Nureyev coruscated at the expense of everything else . . . He and Fonteyn might have been creatures from two different planets.' He found it 'a quite unmoving occasion'. *The Times*, while praising the dancing, objected strongly to the changes in the choreography, especially the (now widely adopted) entrechats in Act II. Both the *Telegraph* and the *Financial Times* revised their opinions after a few more performances. By the autumn *The Times* was writing 'The partnership between these two can be accounted among the noblest in history'.

The rather confused reception after the London première was transformed to enthusiasm when the pair made their American début in the ballet the next spring. 'In all its many years it has not been vested with any greater honour bestowed upon it [than that] by Dame Margot Fonteyn (in the title part) together with one of the greatest Albrechts of all time, Rudolf Nureyev,' wrote the *Herald Tribune* critic. Recalling that formerly Fonteyn's Giselle had been 'complete but not satisfactory', he now considered 'she could, with all honesty be classed with the world's greatest actors . . . a portrayal never to be forgotten by those privileged to see it.' 'If it was really Mr Nureyev who caused her to dance as she did in *Giselle*, he should certainly be her partner all the time,' agreed the *New York Times*. But although admiring his 'incontestably triumphant dancing', this paper did not care for his Albrecht, 'an affected, almost effeminate character'.

Nureyev's supple style (and his long hair) were to continue to arouse critical misgivings in some quarters, but the triumph of the partnership was never in doubt. The *New York Dance News* echoed both the plaudits, and the fears. 'Certain technical feats [of Fonteyn] . . . suddenly took on a new ease and brilliance. At a period in her career when she might understandably have begun to rely on her reputation and the loyal love of audiences she was earning fresh and deserved triumphs for every appearance. For this Nureyev is surely responsible. The partnership is a dazzling and also a moving one. His dancing often comes close to the incredible. He creates a new dimension in dance. It is beyond technique and indescribable.' But again disturbing doubts arose. 'Nureyev will never be just another member of the Royal Ballet or any other.'

In later years they were to repeat their triumph with other companies. 'They are the embodiment of romantic fire and melancholy while continuing to enact the story with a simplicity of mind which owes nothing to convention,' *Le Figaro* wrote in 1965. 'With them every movement of the body is transmuted into fear, hope, a surge of passion or despair.' 'Yesterday I seemed to "read" *Giselle* for the first time,' said *Le Monde* about the same performances. 'Thanks to these two exceptional protagonists the melodrama, the stereotyped and maudlin immaturity, the elements of the quaint and the fey which often disfigure Adam's old ballet completely fell away.' Two years later the *Kronenzeitung* described a performance in Vienna. 'The art of Fonteyn and Nureyev reaches metaphysical heights. It sends shudders down the spine and brings tears to the eyes.' In Spain the story was the same. 'Nureyev moves and dances with an elegance and allure that could not be guessed from watching him on film or television,' wrote *La Vanguardia* in 1968. 'Margot Fonteyn is a ballerina of the first rank and in *Giselle* she proved it completely.' 'Nureyev seems to raise Margot Fonteyn with his eyes alone,' wrote *Le Figaro* that year, 'wafting her into space . . . before letting her vanish into the darkness like a sigh.'

Jacques Loyau

Judy Cameron

With Leslie Edwards as Hilarion and
Gerd Larsen as Giselle's mother

Keith Money

Swan Lake

First performance together Nervi, 5 July, 1962
Choreography Marius Petipa/Lev Ivanov **Music** Pyotr Tchaikovsky
Design Leslie Hurry

THE COMING together of Fonteyn and Nureyev in *Swan Lake* was inevitable, but clearly fraught with dangers and difficulties. It exposed at its highest pitch the difference in background, teaching and experience between the two dancers, and at the same time it offered them the richest field for their gifts.

The ballet itself is a staple part of the repertoire of both the Russian company (for whom it had been arranged in 1895) and the Royal Ballet, which had inherited the version handed down by Nikolai Sergeyev, Diaghilev's old régisseur. Both dancers came to the work with firmly entrenched ideas arising from their different traditions.

Perhaps appropriately, it was the British ballerina who set store on conserving the language of the old production, and the young Russian, fresh from a company in which the classics were constantly revived and renewed, who wished to make changes. He had been impressed by Fonteyn's interpretation of the Royal Ballet version, but felt particularly uncertain about the traditional scenes of pure mime: in Russia these were now always replaced by dancing. 'He thought', Fonteyn has written, that 'he would feel silly standing about doing nothing while I told the story in gesture, and added with a touch of embarrassment, "I am afraid I will ruin your *Swan Lake.*" I looked him straight in the eye and said amiably "Just you try." '

There was much friendly give-and-take between the conflicting approaches. This was perhaps the moment when the mutual respect between the two dancers was sealed. They were both able to defend their ideas with argument and good humour, each clearly learning from the other. The first public try-out of their compromise solution – in which Fonteyn gallantly abandoned her mime (Nureyev was to adopt a version of it later in some productions) – took place on the open-air stage at Nervi in Italy as part of a new festival. They were dancing, not with the senior Royal Ballet, but with its touring company. 'The performances came out beautifully,' Fonteyn recorded.

The *Sunday Telegraph* thought the changes suited Fonteyn 'surprisingly well', but added 'There is obviously a good deal of detail and growing together before this *Swan Lake* will match the Fonteyn–Nureyev *Giselle*. And it may take time for Nureyev's very naturalistic, very soft relaxed style to blend with ours in such a way as not to make us look frigid.'

A German critic, writing in *Die Bühne*, was carried away. 'Margot Fonteyn is not only a brilliant technician, she is one of the most remarkable dancers of our generation – perhaps the most remarkable. The spirituality of her expression blends with Tchaikovsky's music into an inseparable whole. Her movements are of indescribable grace; her virtuosity is stupendous.' As for Nureyev, 'for him the vocabulary of a critic is hardly adequate to suggest the incredible effect which the entrance of the blond, blue-eyed new Nijinsky made on the ecstatic public . . . A happier and more elegant combination than these two overwhelming stars is hardly thinkable.'

The production did not reach London until the following year (7 February 1963), when it had a reception in which rhapsodies about the performance mingled with doubts about the choreography. There was much criticism of the new details introduced by Nureyev: 'Not all the changes were improvements,' noted the *Dancing Times*. 'But there was an exciting feeling that . . . a beginning was being made towards a *Swan Lake* more romantic in feeling and more convincing dramatically. Nureyev plays the Prince with such supple elegance of movement that one is reminded all the time of his incomparable school. Fonteyn has gone a long way towards matching her style to that of Nureyev. The challenge of the occasion and the marvellously sympathetic response from her partner resulted in a fresh and beautifully co-ordinated performance'.

The understanding between the two dancers seemed to reach a peak in this ballet. The smallest nuance of movement evoked an answering response. The dancing poured from them in an unbroken stream leaving at the end a sense of loss as though something unrecapturable had gone. 'Fonteyn, adopting a rather stronger, and tauter tone than formerly, was dancing with marvellous unforced artistry – soft but not soppy as Odette and shining but not hard as Odile,' wrote *The Observer*. 'The final separation of the two lovers was infinitely moving – you could almost hear the sound of tearing as Fonteyn broke from his arms and ran blindly down to the water. Nureyev, partnering with his uncanny mixture of tact and tenderness, was at all times at his classical best . . . He seemed to have all the time in the world. That his sensational solo seemed only an item is a tribute to a dancer who can turn a puppet into a prince and a prince into a poet.'

'A night of delight . . . both dancers were inspired,' exclaimed the *Daily Herald*. 'This is a true partnership when each inspires and strengthens the other,' thought the *Sunday Telegraph*. Even the communist *Daily Worker*, not normally a great admirer of the defected Russian, admitted that 'with Nureyev as her partner Fonteyn seems to grow younger and more relaxed'.

The Guardian found it 'a typical Fonteyn–Nureyev occasion with pyrotechnics for him and quieter activity from her'. The *Financial Times* found Fonteyn 'more magnificent than ever', and Nureyev showing 'all his amazing gifts at their best', but thought his interpretation of Siegfried 'over-youthful and mannered'. *The Times* critic thought the changes from the old production (including the now generally accepted Act I solo) 'an unmitigated disaster', but said of Fonteyn that he 'had never previously been so strongly aware of that suppressed ecstasy which . . . has always given her performance its individuality . . .' *Dance and Dancers* was not at all enthusiastic, except about the last scene. The *Daily Mail* and the *Daily Express* both pointed out the new assurance of Fonteyn's virtuosity: 'She actually stopped the show with her fouettés. I cannot remember this ever happening before,' commented the *Daily Mail*, adding that Nureyev's dancing 'was, of course, spectacular. But perhaps his sincere, natural acting, his gentleness and his ardent longing for Odette were even more remarkable.' The *Daily Express* wrote that 'The Fonteyn–Nureyev team is beyond question one of the glories of British ballet. To the favourite classic it brings a new depth and a new brilliance'.

The Sunday Times actually approved of the new choreography and welcomed 'a new Nureyev, an "English" Nureyev all of our own; a beautifully behaved, modest and controlled Nureyev giving simply and splendidly a well thought-out and carefully rehearsed performance . . . This noble creature, it seems, has been tamed by Fonteyn.' As for the ballerina, 'Watching her sad, pretty face we seem to be experiencing an adventure of the soul.'

Introduced to Paris in the autumn to launch the new Festival de Danse, the traditional production did not please but the stars did. Nureyev was hailed as 'a genius' and of Fonteyn *Arts* wrote: 'The public which had come to see Nureyev made a fool of itself by claiming to "discover" Margot Fonteyn. The fact is that she is one of the two or three greatest living dancers. Her Act II is the finest I have ever seen. She replaces the sophistication usual to superstars by a sort of divine simplicity . . . What can one say of Nureyev? He is today at the height of his form. The way in which he integrates himself with the drama, the smallest of his gestures, are miracles of expressiveness.'

The ballet gave scope for continuous variations in their interpretation over the years; it remained fresh, season after season in country after country. In 1964 they danced together in Nureyev's own version in Vienna. A German critic writing in *Dance and Dancers* considered that 'Fonteyn acquitted herself marvellously in the challenging new task, giving a lesson in purity of style if not actually technique'. Of Nureyev he wrote that 'his dancing was magnificent – the surefootedness of his preparations, the rock-sure endings of his complicated combinations, his marvellously held passés, the sweeping arcs of his leaps, his turns with differentiated speeds – well, one could go on forever.'

Three years later, in New York, critics recorded that while Nureyev stopped the show with his solo, 'it was Fonteyn, dancing with glorious abandon, who dominated this farewell.' In 1972, ten years after their debut together, the *New Yorker* was still crisply enthusiastic: 'Margot Fonteyn is still the champ in the White/Black Swan and Nureyev is the finest partner she ever had.'

Serge Lido

Linda Vartoogian

Judy Cameron

Anthony Crickmay

Mira

Arks Smith

Le Corsaire

First performance together London, 3 November, 1962
Choreography Marius Petipa/Vakhtang Chabukiani **Music** Riccardo Drigo
Design André Levasseur

T HE GRAND pas de deux from Act III of the old Petipa ballet *Le Corsaire* has been a famous bravura piece in the Russian repertory for many years. It stands apart from the rest of the ballet, introducing a character who appears only at this point – a prince who, like the heroine, has been enslaved by the pirate hero of the ballet. Originally the pirate himself took part, but the dance was revised extensively in the first half of this century and became a simple pas de deux – eight minutes of explosive dancing which offer to the girl a part full of vivacious charm and to the man a supreme opportunity to show off his powers – particularly if these include plasticity, generous turns, and a giant jump.

This was the pas de deux which Nureyev had chosen for his prize-winning performance in the students' competition in Moscow – it was to remain one of his specialities – and he taught it to Fonteyn. It is basically just a classical piece with overtones of character; it is the dramatic punch of the choreography – offering openings to vulgar interpretation – and the commonplace music which sometimes lend it a flavour of exaggerated balletic braggadocio.

Its highly charged virtuosity and panache came as a thunderclap on the decorous London dance scene, offering in Nureyev a type and standard of male dancer not seen there for decades and also a new Fonteyn, mischievous, brilliant, apparently revelling in the technical demands of her role. 'The curtain came down at Covent Garden last night to cheers, shouts and flying carnations,' *The Observer* recorded after the première. 'Fonteyn . . . sparkled and spun and dipped like a filly loosed out to grass . . . Nureyev, lithe and hungry-looking in silver trousers, stunned the audience . . . leaping and turning like a salmon, soft as a panther, proud and cruel, never for a moment relaxing his classical control.'

The short fragment, with its oriental aura, Byronic sparkle and romantic fire (Nureyev had richly filled out the academic skeleton) became a universal favourite overnight. They had transformed what can be an empty gala display into a thrilling miniature illustration of that blend of character, technique and style which is the essence of dramatic classical ballet.

Opinion about the occasion was virtually unanimous. 'A triumph of the craft of ballet dancing over the art of ballet', wrote *The Times*, which found the work 'totally unmemorable' but agreed that 'Nureyev danced the piece with a spirit and reverence which would have done credit to a choreographic master-piece', while Fonteyn 'wearing the . . . paste-brilliance with a distinctive assurance, danced with an immense vivacity'. *Dance and Dancers* questioned the place of a pas de deux in an Opera House programme, but felt the occasion had justified it. 'Fonteyn was dancing as well as I have seen her for years, fouettés and all . . . Nureyev was at his most spectacular . . . at his best his stage appearances can be a sublime dance experience – something that happens but rarely in anybody's lifetime.' The *Dancing Times* critic agreed: 'The audi-ence roared because it had seen two great dancers of star quality perform not very interesting steps in an altogether breathtaking way.'

Every critic saluted Fonteyn's vitality (a new facet of her artistic personality) and Nureyev's flaring virtuosity, 'sleek barbarity and magnetic power' (*Daily Express*) and 'leaping like a demented tiger' (*Daily Telegraph*). The *New Statesman* shrewdly noted the Byronic romanticism which Nureyev, uniquely, lent to the bravura steps. 'The fervour and self-assured indifference to conven-tion, the poetic intoxication with violence, were all there.'

Most critics conveyed a sense of slight embarrassment at having enjoyed themselves so much, but *John O'London's* found it 'for all its emphasis on display, a rare *objet d'art* . . . The greatest splendour of the Fonteyn–Nureyev partnership is the way in which Nureyev releases in Fonteyn the joy of dancing . . . Together, in a trifle, they are ballet's most perfect partnership, a non-pareil achievement in dance.'

In America, even six years later, the impact of the tiny piece was as powerful as ever. 'The excitement of the season so far', wrote a New York critic in the *Dancing Times* 'is Nureyev in *Le Corsaire* . . . an elemental creature of primitive power harnessed to the discipline of a prodigious technique.'

Their achievement in this work is preserved in the film 'An Evening with the Royal Ballet'.

Leslie Spatt

Zoë Dominic

Zoë Dominic

Judy Cameron

Anthony Crickmay

Les Sylphides

First performance together London, 6 November, 1962
Choreography Michel Fokine **Music** Frédéric Chopin
Design Alexandre Benois

T HE BRIEF suite of dream-like moonlit dances first devised by Fokine for a
charity performance in St Petersburg under the title 'Chopiniana' and later
introduced to the West by Diaghilev as *Les Sylphides*, has proved more resistant
to mortality than most solid and elaborate full-length productions. It has been
in the repertoire of the Royal Ballet almost since the company's inception, and
was revived with care in 1955 by Grigoriev, Diaghilev's own régisseur. Nureyev,
too, was familiar with it in Leningrad. He and Fonteyn came together in it nine
months after their first appearance together.

It was the rather unusual combination of the Prelude and the pas de deux
which Fonteyn danced with Nureyev at Covent Garden. Her softly flowing style
and tender, melancholy features were ideal for the ballet. Nureyev danced the
solo (normal in Russia, and Fokine's original version) to the Op. 33 Mazurka,
slightly more demanding technically than the solo usually performed in the
West. The role of the Poet is notoriously difficult – a combination of soft
strength and mystical romanticism. Nureyev seemed to grasp the style instinctively. '*Les Sylphides* is a ballet I rarely danced because I have never really had a
clear understanding of it,' Fonteyn said once. 'Nureyev made it quite clear in his
interpretation.'

The production was rapturously received, both stars sharing in the praise. Of
Fonteyn, *The Times* wrote: 'She now appears as a fugitive vision, more ethereal
spirit than frail muse. This conception, so much in accord with Fokine's own,
has found a perfect match in Mr Nureyev. At the end of the ballet a sudden shaft
of bewilderment strikes [him] and with a slight movement of the head he seems
to evoke all the poets who have ever seen visions. They danced supremely well
together, caught up in the same music, borne along on the same stream.' A
writer in *The Observer* described (a year later) how 'Nureyev listens, unheedful
of himself, as though drunk with visions of moonlight . . . His movement is
never obtrusive and enormous leaps flow quite naturally from his modest ac-
tions.' *Dance and Dancers* described Fonteyn as 'seeming to tremble in the
breeze like a flower . . . Here was a ballerina for Pushkin to write about and of
course Nureyev was Pushkin'. *The Dancing Times* found in Fonteyn 'an elegiac
loveliness'. It seemed truly that, as *Dance and Dancers* wrote, 'This performance deserves to become legendary.'

One critic was not carried away. 'Fonteyn, wearing her Chinese expression,
danced the Prelude most delicately,' he wrote in *The Sunday Times*. 'She and
Nureyev made their exits at the end of the pas de deux a bar or two too soon.
And Nureyev, kneeling at the finish of his Mazurka, waited a second too long
and in vain for the Muse to inspire him what to do with his hands.' Six months
later a writer in the *Dancing Times* raised a different objection. It reported that
Grigoriev had said that, though Nureyev was the only dancer in his experience
comparable to Nijinsky, and that he found him incomparable in the ballet,
he still thought he did not seem quite the Poet which Fokine intended – 'his personality is too exotic – too feline'. Future generations will be able to judge for
themselves, for the production is included in the film 'An Evening with the
Royal Ballet'.

Marguerite and Armand

First performance together London, 3 March, 1963
Choreography Frederick Ashton **Music** Franz Liszt
Design Cecil Beaton

IN THE autumn of 1962 the public learned that Ashton was working on a ballet based on Dumas' famous novel *La Dame aux Camélias*. Fonteyn was to be the consumptive courtesan, Nureyev the adoring and adored lover. Already a romantic vehicle for many stars of stage and screen, this work was now to be the frame for ballet's most famous lovers.

Ashton had been nursing the project for many years; now the players and the music (heard by accident on the radio) suddenly presented themselves. Rehearsals began to an accompaniment of feverish curiosity by the Press. Finally a date was set for the première, 13 December.

The report that Nureyev had been taken ill, that there was no question of a substitute and the première would be postponed and the programme revised, created a stir like, as *Dance and Dancers* complained, 'a government reshuffle'. Eventually on an evening in March the curtain went up on a ballet which was to become to the public the epitome of the Fonteyn–Nureyev partnership.

Ashton, normally the maestro of delicacy and restraint, had plunged wholeheartedly into the hot emotionalism of the nineteenth-century melodrama. Compressing the story with skill and deploying shrewdly the appearance and personalities of his two stars, he squeezed the whole action into a series of tense, highly charged scenes. 'For Fonteyn I think *Marguerite and Armand* may be said to extend her range of performing,' said Ashton. 'Not as a dancer, but it does demand more of her acting than any other roles except Giselle. Nureyev is a marvellous artist and a considerable theatre personality. He's a good Armand because he's romantic and passionate. As for the two, together in my ballet they create an air of great love.'

Pressure-cooked melodrama is not made for repeated viewing and Ashton's contribution to the success of the production was unjustly decried in some quarters in later years. But at the time doubts were thrown to the wind. 'In spite of the 10,000 spring carnations which happily bedecked Covent Garden for its royal gala last night, one felt it should have been camellias, camellias all the way,' wrote *The Times*. 'In essence his [Ashton's] work is nothing more than a decorated pas de deux for Marguerite and Armand, and that proves abundant enough . . . The swiftness of the ballet gives it a hallucinatory quality and sense of flying passion, of a tragedy fitfully illuminated by flashes of Keats' "spangly doom" . . . Here is the true Romantic agony distilled into a brief ballet, far more pungent in its effect than any *Giselle* . . . Dame Margot Fonteyn, ranging from nervous gaiety to mask-like tragedy, with emotion ebbing and flowing in her features and dancing more with her heart than her feet, is the Lady of the Camellias to the life. Yet to an extent it remains Mr Nureyev's ballet. Here is an Armand of wild dreams, fierce authority and depths of feeling the choreography can plumb but not fully chart.'

The *Financial Times*, noting the acute sense of period of the acting, found it 'an amazingly exciting work – a study in blazing emotion that is unique in Ashton's output. Fonteyn gives a performance of lambent beauty that is matched by the fervour of Nureyev . . . A work to see again and again, to treasure.' Two years later, a different writer in the same paper thought it 'revealed a new Fonteyn, passionate, violent, reckless and for her he [Ashton] has created his most concise and emotional work . . . A daydream is conveyed in a gesture and a month of happiness in a few bars.'

There were reservations. The *Daily Mail* objected that the ballet revealed no new aspects of the dancers. The *Daily Telegraph* thought it worked 'only by a prodigious outburst of mutually inspired and totally extrovert acting'. The *Scotsman* recorded 'virtuoso interpretations of a high order' but no emotional response. *The Guardian*, however, while judging the whole work 'a glaring example of trespass' on other media, literary and operatic, saw in Nureyev's part 'an aspect of his great talent which is not unknown but is rather less familiar than his virtuosity. It has provided too, and perhaps more surprisingly, a dramatic Fonteyn.' *The Stage* thought the event justified the means. 'Never has Nureyev's humanity glowed so warmly. Never has Fonteyn's grief been so heart-rending. Some may consider it an old-fashioned ballet to be creating in 1963. Who cares?'

Enthusiasm easily won the day. *The Sunday Times* found the ballet 'a tremendous vehicle for the special gifts of Fonteyn and Nureyev. I cannot imagine anyone else doing it. By special gifts I mean this. Fonteyn's genius is for the expression of emotion, chiefly with her face and arms. And Nureyev, a dancer of splendid nerve and dash, has much greater potentialities . . . as an expressive artist. His characterization of Armand, in turn gay, impassioned, cruel and heart-broken is much the best thing that he has done.'

The Observer celebrated the occasion by recalling its one-time ballet critic Peter Brook, who had not written about dance for fifteen years. He wrote: 'In *Marguerite and Armand* over the music Ashton improvises freely, composing a floating line of melody all his own, closely related to Liszt's score yet utterly independent, and in this respect the work is simple, beautiful and satisfying. Its transparency is such that Ashton can even permit himself the audacity of stillness – the breath is caught, the gestures suspended in pauses which, like the silence of Marguerite Duras, are as lyrical as any steps . . . In this ballet Nureyev and Fonteyn play as actors; extraordinary actors who bring to each moment and each movement that quality of death which makes the most artificial of forms seem human and simple. All great art eventually is realistic; the art of these two dancers leads them continually to moments of truth.'

Anglo-EMI film still

Left: with Leslie Edwards as the Duke in a film production

Keith Money

Zoë Dominic

Frederika Davis

Zoë Dominic

With Michael Somes as Armand's father

Zoë Dominic

Keith Money

116 Marguerite and Armand

Zoë Dominic

Keith Money

Beverley Gallegos

Anthony Crickmay

Houston Rogers

Symphonic Variations

First performance together London, 1 April, 1963
Choreography Frederick Ashton **Music** César Frank
Design Sophie Federovitch

MOST COMPANIES have in their repertoire a ballet which becomes something of a 'signature work' – a piece which sums up its special qualities. For the Royal Ballet this has for many years been a short abstract ballet by Frederick Ashton, *Symphonic Variations*.

It was created in 1946, only two months after the company had moved into its new home at Covent Garden. Its small scale – it employs only six dancers – may bear the imprint of Ashton's long experience on a smaller stage, but it proved able to fill the opera house amply through its sheer intensity of mood. From the first, Fonteyn had been both its centrepiece and, it appeared, its inspiration. Its qualities were her qualities and it was a perfect example of the way in which the style of the whole company had been moulded around hers. An exercise in delicate classicism, its lyrical purity seemed to sum up the 'English style', with its emphasis on reticence, finesse, perfect finish and a quiet pastoral lyricism.

The prospect of Nureyev, the emblem of a fundamentally different culture, stepping into this almost sacred sextet seemed alarming. His first (and last) appearance in the ballet took place only a few weeks after the première of *Marguerite and Armand*, a work in which Ashton had positively exploited his tempestuous individuality.

'To some extent it is to us what *The Sleeping Beauty* is to the Kirov Ballet', wrote *The Times* next morning. 'It may possibly not be our best ballet but it is undeniably our most characteristic. Into such a private world Mr Nureyev enters as a welcome stranger. Yet perhaps not as strange as that, for his Kirov schooling has much in common with the Royal Ballet, and it was a particular joy to see how well he fitted into our ensemble. His ports de bras were more romantic in their feeling, more calculatedly negligent in their pose, but this seemed of supremely small account.'

'There was an extraordinary potency about his restraint,' wrote *The Guardian*. 'The familiar pantherine quality was there but it was, if anything, more impressive for being latent rather than exuberant. Of Fonteyn's perform-ance there can be no higher praise than that she was, last night, as she always has been in this most Fonteynesque ballet.'

Considering the pursed lips which had greeted Nureyev's ventures into some of the Royal Ballet repertoire, the comments were remarkably favourable. 'Never once stepping out of line, he nevertheless managed to add a personal touch of glamour to his dancing that added to its effectiveness,' wrote *Dance and Dancers*, while the *Spectator*, remarking that he was 'jumping in on a Royal Ballet rite where almost angels might fear to tread', judged that 'the nature of his success was such that, whenever he seemed out of place, it also forced one to put the place-cards of his colleagues in doubt.'

For all his restraint, Nureyev's deep, almost mystical, ecstasy was not in the cool anonymous mood customary in this ballet, and some thought that even Fonteyn had changed. 'Something of this emotional dimension . . . seemed to transfer itself to Fonteyn,' wrote one critic. 'She adds a certain rapt quality that, to be perhaps fanciful, has a happy air of sainthood about it. The impassive delicacy has thawed into positive serenity.' There was no doubt that this was a more highly charged occasion than the ballet normally produced – or perhaps aimed at. It was to remain an isolated performance. The only surviving record is a rehearsal picture, with Georgina Parkinson and Ann Jenner.

La Sylphide

First performance together Athens, 9 August, 1963
Choreography August Bournonville **Music** Herman Løvenskjold
Design Eugène Lami/Peter Rice

ORIGINALLY created in Paris in 1832, *La Sylphide* has survived mainly in the version re-choreographed by August Bournonville for the Royal Danish Ballet. The most celebrated modern exponent of its male role, the Danish Erik Bruhn, taught it to Nureyev soon after the Russian's arrival in the West, and when Fonteyn was compiling a programme for the group which she took on tour in 1963, he produced the final scene as a pas de deux. It was repeated in London at the Royal Academy of Dancing gala at Drury Lane on 6 December.

The lyrical dancing assigned to the Sylph suited Fonteyn to perfection, and her sad farewell to her Scottish lover gave moving scope for her gentle acting; while Nureyev obviously revelled in the change from the broad, emotionally charged Russian style to Bournonville's clean, quick, mercurial choreography.

'Both were superb in catching the romantic feeling of the ballet and its style,' wrote *The Times* after the London performance. *The Observer* thought that 'Fonteyn made a moving spirit, bang in the period as the tragic, unattainable dream-woman, while Nureyev, spruce and bonny in a kilt, gave the bouncy Bournonville choreography new life with plastic body-movements linked to beats as sharp and dangerous as Highland dirks.' The *Daily Mail* found Nureyev 'at his springiest, lightest best', while *The Sunday Times* thought both he and Fonteyn had 'entirely captured the elusive style of Bournonville'. Both the *Financial Times* and *The Sunday Times* looked forward to seeing them together in the complete ballet.

Nureyev did go on to dance the complete ballet with several companies. 'His first James in New York was unquestionably superb,' wrote the *New York Times* when he appeared as the hero of the ballet in America ten years later. 'He adopts the Bournonville style literally like a native. This was an absolutely superlative reading of this great and classic Danish role.' But Fonteyn did not return to it – a neglect which many of her admirers have much regretted.

G B L Wilson

Gayane

First performance together Athens, 9 August, 1963
Choreography Nina Anisimova **Music** Aram Khachaturian
Design Natan Altman/Peter Rice

NUREYEV had been familiar with the full-length *Gayane* since his student days in Leningrad (he had danced a solo from it in the Moscow competition), and he taught the 'Kurdish' pas de deux to Fonteyn for the 1963 Royal Academy of Dancing gala at Drury Lane. However, he was ultimately unable to dance in the gala because of a foot injury, and Fonteyn was partnered by a former fellow pupil of Nureyev's, a Hungarian dancer now working in Budapest, Viktor Rona.

The duet was a big success, and it was introduced into the repertoire of a touring group organized by Fonteyn the next summer. Curiously, it was never repeated, except in a BBC television programme the following November which launched a new series called 'Gala Performance'. The television critic of *Dance and Dancers* found Fonteyn 'charming and gay' in the number. 'The *demi-caractère* nature of it suited her and the suggestions of oriental movements were brought off to perfection . . . Nureyev now adds to the gaiety and excitement. Some of the pas de deux they give are slightly unbalanced, for virtuosity is his forte while it has never really been hers . . . In this, however, they are perfectly balanced, Fonteyn matching his soaring leaps by perfect timing, speed and charm.'

Zoë Dominic

La Bayadère

First performance together London, 27 November, 1963
Choreography Marius Petipa/Rudolf Nureyev **Music** Ludwig Minkus
Design Philip Prowse

WHEN THE Kirov Ballet visited the West in 1962, one of its showpieces was an extract from the old Petipa ballet *La Bayadère* – one of the vision scenes often inserted into long works to show off the classical paces of a company. Nureyev was to have starred in it when the company came to London. Instead, he later mounted the short scene known as *The Kingdom of the Shades* for the Royal Ballet, with himself and Fonteyn taking the central roles – his first real effort at choreography and the first evidence of his phenomenal memory.

Doubts were felt in some quarters about the wisdom of entrusting this pure classical pearl to a young man who had already shown that he was not afraid to make alterations to well-loved choreography. But fears faded when the curtain rose on what turned out to be an almost exact reconstruction of the original. The main alterations were a new ending borrowed from another part of the ballet and a change in the placing of the male solo (which was already an interpolation from an earlier act). There were also some changes in minor details, such as the 'parallel' steps for hero and heroine in the famous scarf duet. Most of these were accepted as improvements.

By tradition the work is a showpiece for the corps de ballet, and so it was eventually to become for the Royal Ballet. But at the première attention was focused on the two stars and here some nervousness took the edge off what was later to become a triumphant display of classical prowess. In his first solo Nureyev, miscalculating the size of the stage, jumped himself virtually off it, a scene vividly described by the *Bristol Evening Post*. 'Tension at the Royal Opera House. Rudolf Nureyev, half-way through his first production there, does a tremendous turn in the air and makes a false landing. He rushes into the wings. The ballet goes on, but hardly anyone in the crowded house notices. They are waiting to see if their Russian favourite is hurt. Three minutes pass, and back he comes like a tornado, with even more astonishing leaps and turns. When it is all over the audience roar their relief.'

The Guardian greeted the work as 'a kind of landmark in the story of the Royal Ballet' with Fonteyn 'dauntless, cool and regal as she always is in Nureyev's company'. *The Times* wrote 'Fonteyn's fleet footwork and exquisite placing invested her dancing with a combination of breadth and elegance', while Nureyev, 'beturbaned and beplumed, shot through the ballet like an arrow'.

The *Financial Times* proclaimed the ballet 'a lasting monument to the undying values of classical dance . . . We expected Nureyev to shine and shine he did in two prodigious variations . . . but it was Fonteyn who dazzled even more. This was Fonteyn the superlative stylist and also Fonteyn the amazing technician, dancing with extraordinary speed and assurance.' *Dance and Dancers*, reflecting a few weeks later, remarked that the ballet 'provided what was virtually a quantitive check on Fonteyn's physical prowess . . . The ballet exploited a whole technical armoury that one hardly knew she possessed.' Of Nureyev in the ballet this critic wrote 'There is a most remarkable intensity about his stage personality that electrifies an audience even before he starts to dance . . . As a technician British ballet has never seen his like . . . With *La Bayadère* he has presented us with a great classic to cherish and, what is equally important, taught us how to dance it. If he were to fly away tomorrow, he has already now achieved enough to ensure that British ballet will be forever in his debt.' The *New*

Daily, equally impressed, wrote simply: 'Nureyev has offered the Royal Ballet a jewel and they wear it as jewels should be worn, proudly and with beauty.'

There were a few dissenting voices. The *Daily Telegraph*, under the heading 'Quaint Hindu Fable Ballet', summed it up as 'an historical curiosity' and the *Daily Worker*, the London communist paper, found the whole ballet merely 'old fashioned and very, very dull'.

The reception of the ballet's première in New York later in the year (led by two resident Royal Ballet dancers) was decidedly muted. The *New York Times* critic contented himself with remarking 'unfortunately the corps de ballet did poorly', though he found the 'second performance better with Fonteyn and Nureyev'. Today, *La Bayadère* is a favourite with New York audiences, and has been mounted by American Ballet Theatre. In London its popularity endures, with the corps de ballet as of yore the star of the production.

Frederika Davis

Keith Money

Zoë Dominic

Divertimento

First performance together Bath, 9 June, 1964
Choreography Kenneth MacMillan **Music** Béla Bartók
Design Barry Kay

FOR THE Bath Music Festival of 1964 its Director, Yehudi Menuhin, suggested that Fonteyn and Nureyev perform a duet. Kenneth MacMillan agreed to choreograph it, and the music chosen was Bartók's Sonata for solo violin, to be played by Menuhin himself.

It was never intended to be more than a *pièce d'occasion*, but it entered ballet history through the circumstances of its birth. The night before the performance Fonteyn received news from Panama that her husband had been shot in the street and wounded. At first the news seemed reassuring, and she decided to carry on with the performance and fly out to her husband next day.

Her anxiety did not show in her dancing of the short pas de deux – a sequence of twisting, faltering movements in which Nureyev seemed to take the lead, hinting perhaps (so one critic said) at Orpheus leading Eurydice through limbo. The *Glasgow Herald* found it 'rather thin, being no more than a pas de deux made for the dancers and as disposable as a paper cup'. And *Dance and Dancers*, seeing images of 'encounter, searching and flight, perhaps even blindness', thought the choreography too slow-paced to be expressive. But the *Bath Weekly Chronicle* found it 'the artistic summit of the whole festival . . . the movement matched the sad, meandering music to the last nuance, the final half-tone. But it was the complete entity of the two which drew magic out of the mime and music.'

The Observer thought 'The presence and playing of . . . Yehudi Menuhin certainly contributed much; the dancing of the extraordinary couple contributed more; but the most credit must go to the choreographer', while the *Daily Telegraph* thought its 'gravely beautiful choreography' was 'the triumph of the evening', and the audience loved it, demanding (and getting) a complete encore. But it was never to be repeated.

Raymonda

First performance together Spoleto, 19 July, 1964
Choreography Marius Petipa/Rudolf Nureyev **Music** Alexander Glazunov
Design Beni Montresor

O F ALL THE full-length ballets made by Petipa in Russia, only *The Sleeping Beauty* and *Swan Lake* are widely familiar in the West. But another of his major productions which has survived in Russia is virtually unknown elsewhere, *Raymonda*. In 1964, Nureyev was commissioned to reconstruct it from his memories of the Leningrad production for the Royal Ballet's touring section. It was premièred at the Spoleto Festival in Italy.

After an absence at the bedside of her wounded husband, Fonteyn joined the company to take the principal role opposite Nureyev. But at the very last minute, just before the final dress rehearsal, she received a message that her husband had had a relapse. Within half an hour she was on her way to London, and Doreen Wells was hurriedly rehearsing to replace her the next day.

The production – Nureyev's first major undertaking – understandably proved only partially successful. The ballet itself suffered from an impossibly awkward libretto, a mishmash of the medieval crusade motifs fashionable when it was written (1898). But 'By reducing the story to its bare essentials and eliminating nearly all the mime Nureyev gave us in effect an abstract ballet of sheer glorious dancing,' said the *Dancing Times*. 'Nureyev has boldly set out to minimize the work's faults by simply ignoring them,' agreed *Dance and Dancers*, which felt the solution unsatisfactory. 'However, the dances are so exquisitely varied and buoyantly, assertively choreographed that no one is likely to complain. Doreen Wells, jumping into the breach sadly left by Fonteyn, sparkled delightfully as Raymonda . . . If Nureyev was weighed down with responsibility he rose above it. His partnering of Wells was considerate and his solo dancing, swift and aerial, was at its unrivalled spiritual best.'

Fonteyn was able to return to Italy for the final performance and travelled on with the production to the Baalbek Festival. Her first sustained encounter with the incredibly taxing role came the next year when she danced in the revised version which Nureyev arranged for the Australian Ballet. It was premièred in Britain, in Birmingham, on 14 December, with new designs by Ralph Koltai; 'Fonteyn's *Raymonda*, is that an unfair way to think of it?' asked *Dance and Dancers* afterwards. 'Of course it is, and yet in a sense to think of the whole ballet just in the light . . . of Fonteyn's performance is to realize what the whole thing is about. The role shows off to perfection the virtues of the ballerina worthy of it. Fonteyn assumes it with daring, wears it with grace and warms it with majesty.' Of Nureyev – he had built himself a relatively modest part – it remarked that he was 'dancing effortlessly and conveying both in movement and repose the very spirit of courtly love. In the duets Nureyev and Fonteyn are as one.'

Both dancers were to earn high praise when the ballet went on tour in Europe. 'The Russian with the gloriously trained body and the face of a young man out of Pushkin which mirrors untamed nature and raw emotion, drove the public to jubilation,' wrote a Berlin critic. 'Margot Fonteyn is completely sure in her technique in *Giselle* and had, if possible, an even greater success in *Raymonda*.' But the somewhat unwieldy work was not taken into the Royal Ballet repertoire (Nureyev was to mount it in America later), apart from the last act with its lively Hungarian dances – a short version in which the two partners appeared together many times.

Daniel Candé

Jennie Walton

Leslie Spatt

Hamlet

First performance together Baalbek, 25 July, 1964
Choreography Robert Helpmann **Music** Pyotr Tchaikovsky
Design Leslie Hurry

ROBERT HELPMANN's ballet *Hamlet* is a dance-drama with the accent on drama. Using Tchaikovsky's overture as a basis, Helpmann compressed the whole action into a dream, a Freudian nightmare which flashes through Hamlet's mind as he lies dying. The ballet was launched in 1942, with Fonteyn as the gentlest, most touching Ophelia.

The emphasis was firmly on the protagonist. 'There is nothing in the role of Ophelia to warrant bothering a ballerina of the stature of Fonteyn with it,' remarked *Theatre World* after the première. 'Though needless to say she invests it with a poignant charm and pathos.' Other writers described her as 'tender', 'delicate', 'exquisite', even 'douce'. 'When Helpmann as Hamlet manhandles Ophelia in a manner faintly recalling the once notorious Danse des Apaches, one does not resent it, though one may pity Margot Fonteyn, especially as she has developed a peculiarly appealing quality in her mime,' wrote *Time and Tide*. Later it was transferred into the repertoire of the touring section of the Royal Ballet, but it was revived for the main company in 1964 as part of the national celebrations of Shakespeare's quater-centenary, with Nureyev as Hamlet and Lynn Seymour as Ophelia.

Nureyev slipped into the role of Hamlet as if it had been created for him. 'Tremendous, dead right,' thought *The Sunday Times*. 'A natural for the part; his slight, sinewy figure and mobile face responded to every action,' wrote the *Scotsman*. 'Probably his best role so far with the company,' thought the *Daily Telegraph*. 'It is a part which has been waiting for Nureyev and he takes it over with a deathly authority,' wrote *The Observer*, while the *Spectator* pronounced it 'Instantly the most successful ballet of the evening . . . As choreography the ballet scarcely gets to the starting point, but the role of Hamlet, choreographic-ally amplified in this production, offers the dancer a superb opportunity for histrionic attitudinizing. Nureyev . . . was born to play Hamlet and with his sulky magnificence as focus, Helpmann's drama takes on a new, crazy clarity.'

Dance and Dancers considered that 'the reason why Hamlet, with all its faults, emerged stronger at this revival than ever before was almost entirely due to Nureyev's remarkable performance. He broods with glowing intensity. Wild-eyed, lank-haired, hollow-cheeked, he looked the epitome of the self-devouring Prince.' The *Dancing Times* was impressed by Nureyev's 'amazing power but it is his acting which impresses most.' *The Guardian* found him 'admirable . . . His romantic manner and the magnetism of his presence worked wonders.' But the critic still found 'that this very popular little ballet is, as it was twenty years ago, a little monster.'

Fonteyn, the original Ophelia, danced the role opposite the new Hamlet only twice, at the Baalbek Festival in Lebanon; they were never to come together again in the ballet.

Romeo and Juliet

First performance together London, 9 February, 1965
Choreography Kenneth MacMillan **Music** Serge Prokofiev
Design Nicholas Georgiadis

BY 1965 Fonteyn and Nureyev had become fixed in the public mind as the quintessential stage lovers. None the less, their portrayal of Shakespeare's classic pair came about rather awkwardly. Kenneth MacMillan originally devised his version of *Romeo and Juliet* for Lynn Seymour and Christopher Gable, making Juliet the dynamic and dominating motivator of the tragedy, with Romeo as a simple, sympathetic foil. But the management of the company, wishing to take no risks in this major venture, insisted that the première be given to what was unquestionably its top pair.

The story that they were only substituting leaked out and their first performance was given under considerable disadvantages, particularly as Nureyev was suffering from an injury and danced with one leg heavily bandaged. It became clear afterwards (many other couples alternated the parts immediately, including Seymour and Gable) that Fonteyn and Nureyev had given strong personal twists to the roles. In their version Juliet is a tender, immature girl who is driven against her will by her own instincts (Fonteyn lent a moving pathos, gentle but determined, to the scenes with her parents), and Romeo – a somewhat passive and simple-minded character in most versions – was given by Nureyev a mocking, mercurial gaiety which dramatically contrasted with the tragic intensity of his last scenes.

The ballet was received with forty minutes of applause – which was held (by the *Evening Standard*) to constitute a theatrical record. There were a few reservations about the choreography but the designs were highly praised. Critical opinion about the principals was at first divided. *The Times* wrote that Fonteyn, 'with an ecstatic radiance of her own, had a memorable personal victory in choreography not ideally shaped to her image. Mr Rudolf Nureyev, injured but dancing with half a foot better than most men with two, gave a mocking yet ardent Romeo.' The *Daily Telegraph* thought the ballet an achievement of 'solid craftsmanship and organization. Dame Margot and Rudolf Nureyev perform together like a pair of finely adjusted instruments.' *The Guardian* thought 'Fonteyn looked enchantingly, beguilingly young and danced and acted accordingly. This will be one of her greatest interpretations when its details are, here and there, rethought. Nureyev, only slightly inhibited by a foot injury, was, as always, an irresistible eye-catcher – he had more pathos too'. *The Observer*, noting that MacMillan had stressed the private rather than the public tragedy ('love is not so much snuffed between social pressures as bruised to death by life itself'), remarked that Fonteyn brought to her role an 'inimitable mixture of elegance and naïveté; even in the nursery she has an aristocratic delicacy. Though she graduates rather abruptly from dolls to guys, her divided loyalty to her parents and her lover is childlike and clear.' The writer thought that the dances for Romeo were 'mainly in the light, quick tempi which inspire dexterity *à l'anglaise* rather than broad movements expressive of a big manly heart.'

There were some reservations about both dancers. The *New Statesman* praised Nureyev but found that 'Fonteyn started with kitten flirtatiousness and a fine excitement; but once she had fallen in love with Romeo, once she had grown up, she lost track of the character.' The *Financial Times*, on the other hand, praised Fonteyn but criticized Nureyev 'with his untidy hair and floppy smock he never began to have the measure of Romeo.' The *Sunday Telegraph* was also critical, finding Fonteyn's 'gentleness, radiance and puppylove resolution and courage distinctly non-sexual' while the 'tumultuous feelings and energy' of Nureyev's Romeo were too audience-directed – not to mention the offence of 'the scruffiest hairstyle'. *The Listener* went so far as to find both dancers 'a little miscast'. This judgement was gallantly withdrawn after the next performance.

Nureyev's hair, a positive obsession in some quarters, also worried the *Dancing Times*, which was 'enchanted' by Fonteyn but wrote of Nureyev that 'all that is wrong with his Romeo was his hair . . . Otherwise I thought him a little short of magnificent.' A month later, after seeing other interpreters it found that 'the least stimulating of the four pairs has been the first', not through lack of merit but 'precisely because – by being so starrily characteristic it caused the least surprise.' *Dance and Dancers* added that 'perhaps it is the grand manner approach with Fonteyn (and Nureyev) which has upset so many people. Obviously Lynn Seymour is more MacMillan's Juliet, just as Gable is more his Romeo.'

The critical reception in America, which had no inside knowledge of casting problems, was very different, though the public's enthusiasm was the same. The *New York Journal* said: 'the kind of perfection in movement that they achieve together epitomizes the freedom that lies beyond technical mastery. It expresses itself as poetic lyricism.' The *Herald Tribune*, under the heading 'Fabled Pair Fabulous in Royal Ballet', was moved by the acting as much as the dancing and recorded that 'the ovation at the close lasted for over thirty minutes'. The *New York Times* wrote that 'Although Mr Nureyev and Dame Margot were in the spotlight throughout, it was not really a star attraction but rather a production that focused on the whole company'. Another writer in the same paper a few weeks later thought 'It was a joy to see two dancers of such celebrity integrate themselves so completely with the total fabric of the work . . . The entire performance was virtually flawless.' In Britain too, as often happens, reservations were withdrawn as the interpretations developed and critics became tuned in. By 1976 a drama critic writing in the *New Statesman* opined that Fonteyn has 'demonstrated that what makes her unique as a dancer is that she is one of the greatest actresses of her time' while Nureyev was described by *The Times* as 'quite simply incomparable as the mercurial Romeo . . .' and by the *Financial Times* as 'as perfect a Romeo as I hope to see.' It may be that the interpretation had really tightened up.

Frederika Davis

Mike Davis

Frederika Davis

With David Blair as Mercutio and
Gerd Larsen as the nurse

Film still by courtesy of the Rank Organisation Ltd

With Ronald Hynd as the priest

Houston Rogers

Zoë Dominic

Paquita

First performance together London, 17 November, 1965
Choreography Marius Petipa **Music** Edouard Deldevez/Léon Minkus
Design Philip Prowse

IN 1965 Nureyev mounted – for Fonteyn's gala in aid of the Royal Academy of
Dancing – the *grand pas* from the old Petipa ballet *Paquita*, a full-length work
created in 1847 in the Spanish style popular at that time. In the divertissement
four soloists joined Fonteyn and Nureyev in a pas de deux supported by pupils
from the Royal Ballet School. Like all Petipa choreography it demands a perfection of execution beyond the reach of students, and like all charity shows, little
time was available for rehearsal. The number made, as a result, only a mildly
pleasing effect.

'An interesting curiosity rather than one which should take its place in the
repertory of our companies,' thought *Dance and Dancers*, complaining that
most of the revivals of old Petipa works 'looked much alike'. 'Nor somehow
did the principal roles particularly suit Fonteyn and Nureyev, but possibly she
had to give so much time to organizing the performance and he had to give so
much time to getting everyone else on in the ballet that there was little time for
their own performances.' It was judged on the whole to be 'an effective party
piece', but was not accepted into the Royal Ballet repertoire. When, however,
the Kirov company presented it during its London visit in 1970, it proved very
popular. 'A joy', remarked *The Observer*.

Jennie Walton

Frederika Davis

Jennie Walton

Frederika Davis

The Sleeping Beauty

First performance together London, 26 December, 1966
Choreography Marius Petipa **Music** Pyotr Tchaikovsky
Design Oliver Messel

Since its earliest years, the Royal Ballet has treasured *The Sleeping Beauty* as a carefully preserved legacy from the Maryinsky (handed down by Sergeyev). It was the ballet with which the company, led by Fonteyn, opened its Covent Garden career and then, three years later, took New York by storm. Curiously, it was not until relatively late in the history of their partnership that Fonteyn, for whom *The Sleeping Beauty* had always been the brightest setting, and Nureyev, whose interpretation of the Prince in the same work had been one of his most triumphant achievements in Russia, came together in the ballet. Curiously too, the event was almost camouflaged. It took place unassumingly the day after Christmas – when many of the regular audience and most critics are on holiday.

Since Nureyev joined the company, Fonteyn had danced in the ballet many times, but partnered by David Blair; while Nureyev had taken the role of the Prince opposite Nadia Nerina. It was not until 1966 that they joined forces in it – and even then the conjunction seems not to have been altogether smooth. The *Daily Telegraph* thought Fonteyn 'unable to project the character of Princess Aurora fluently because of the faulty partnering of Nureyev'. The *Daily Express* found 'the partnership oddly uneasy, with Nureyev keeping a remote distance from all that went on around him'. *The Stage* praised Fonteyn's 'delicacy and precision' and thought Nureyev 'splendidly groomed and looking every inch a fairy-tale prince' but found in the final pas de deux 'less than the expected brilliance.' *The Observer* had hard words for the twenty-seven-year-old production (soon to be replaced) and though the writer thought that together the two stars 'managed to work up moments of real emotion', he was guarded about their individual performances.

The Times was more favourable. 'Putting together their two very different approaches which, with a little simplification, may be defined as respectively classical and romantic, resulted in a performance that was less than academically correct but far more stimulating than correctiveness could ever be.' The writer welcomed a greater allure in the 'Vision' and more panache in the 'Wedding' scenes. 'Against these virtues a slight lack of polish in the final duet assumes less importance.'

The fact was that in this traditional production the Prince had little dancing and his character was not developed. The hero and heroine do not meet until three-quarters of the way through the ballet and then pass directly into the festivities in the ballroom. The pas de deux from this scene became a regular gala showpiece, but its unemotional choreography was never to give scope for the intense and intimate give-and-take of the finest partnering. In later performances they worked out a harmonious interpretation, with special emphasis on the 'Vision' scene when Fonteyn's ethereal serenity and Nureyev's ardent expressiveness could be given free play.

In 1970, Fonteyn danced in Milan in Nureyev's own majestic version of the ballet. 'In this production the role of the Prince assumes such an importance that it almost eclipses that of Aurora,' wrote a Turin paper after her appearance. 'With the participation of Margot Fonteyn it acquires a just balance, and as a double classical interpretation this was a model hard to beat.' A model of classicism is a fair – and appropriate – summary of their appearance in this ballet.

Keith Money

Paradise Lost

First performance together London, 23 February, 1967
Choreography Roland Petit **Music** Benjamin Constant
Design Martial Raysse

IN 1967 the French choreographer Roland Petit was asked to create a new
ballet for Fonteyn and Nureyev to take to America. Petit had worked
before with Fonteyn, but not with Nureyev. He made a daring proposition: he
suggested breaking away from their accepted image as exponents of traditional
romantic-classicism; instead he would create a ballet in his own version of the
modern style, pitching it in the Pop Art idiom currently in vogue.

As subject Petit chose the Creation, casting the stars as the archetypal couple,
Adam and Eve. For a title he took the name of Milton's poem – a risky
decision as it set up preconceptions which were the very opposite of his inten-
tion and raised in British minds the spectre of disrespect for a beloved
masterpiece.

But shock was manifestly one of Petit's aims. The opening of the ballet – a
countdown flashed in huge neon numbers as if God were launching a missile,
followed by a blinding flash as Adam suddenly appeared inside the primal egg –
set the tone. After a solo by Adam, Eve was born from his side to join him in a
pas de deux, but soon temptation entered in the form of a serpent composed of
men in mauve boiler suits which swallowed her up. In despair, Adam raced
around the stage and finally dived into the mouth of the vast glamour girl
depicted on the backcloth.

Up to this point the ballet, by its inventiveness, the lively beauty of the designs
and the success of the two stars in their novel movements, gripped the audience.
But thereafter the emphasis fell on repetitious manoeuvres for the corps de
ballet and unconvincing suggestions of separation, loneliness and death. Many
of the audience came away disappointed.

Though the work was soon dropped (it received an unenthusiastic response in
America and even in Paris – 'two diamonds in an omelette', remarked
France-Soir) and was later thought of as a misfire, it initially won wide
critical praise. 'Petit, for about half the work, has used this pop-dressed setting
for a quite remarkable series of movements by Nureyev and Fonteyn', wrote the
Dancing Times. 'To Nureyev he has given such original choreography as he has
never had before and he responds superbly.' As for Fonteyn, 'Petit puts her in a
cruelly young, largely unclassical role and she has seldom looked younger or
more seductive or danced with more impeccable timing'.

The Times thought that 'Fonteyn has a role that suits her beautifully and
Nureyev a part that puts his strange, compelling personality to more telling use
than anyone else has succeeded in doing . . . The total effect is natural and
expressive, tremendously exciting to watch, light and amusing and, in the end,
touching too.' The *Financial Times* was even more enthusiastic. 'Adam is a
tremendous role, one that magnificently exploits all the power, grace and
emotion of Nureyev's dancing and one that he dances magnificently – with a
simplicity, a lack of swagger and effortless, undisplayed virtuosity that makes it
seem the finest thing that he has ever done. Fonteyn has possibly not since
Symphonic Variations had so exposed a part composed for her; and she is
amazing. She looks and moves like a young girl. Every movement is expressive,
compelling, revelatory.' A critic in *The Sunday Times* wrote: 'For Fonteyn and
Nureyev, Petit has created something tremendous . . .' *The Observer*, critical of
the second half, liked the opening: 'It is hard to know which to salute more – the
enterprise of Fonteyn in tackling so untypical a role and her complete mastery
of it, or the astonishing range of Nureyev – dramatic, athletic and inimitably

supple in what must be one of the most taxing (and so rewarding) roles in
modern ballet.'

There was some – not much – opposition. The *Daily Express* found the ballet
'glossily chic and at times inventive'. The *Daily Mail* remarked that 'perhaps the
most striking thing – and also the most ugly – is the decor and costumes.' The
Daily Telegraph expressed 'dismay that so complex a work has been assembled
to produce one very simple fact – that Nureyev can dance something other than
stereotypes of classical ballet'. The *Sunday Telegraph* though liking the first
half, doubted if any other dancers could get away with it, while the *Spectator*
dismissed the whole work as 'almost totally insupportable – a marvellously
portrayed bore'.

Anthony Crickmay

Zoë Dominic

Keith Money

Birthday Offering

First performance together London, 29 March, 1968
Choreography Frederick Ashton **Music** Alexander Glazunov
Design André Levasseur

IT SOMETIMES happens that a seemingly careless trifle thrown off for a single occasion lasts better than a solidly planned production. *Birthday Offering* is one of these. Originally composed in 1956 for a gala to celebrate the Royal Ballet's twenty-fifth anniversary, it was designed as an ephemeral diversion to show off the particular qualities of the ballerinas of the day. It was a remarkable tour de force, cunningly ringing the changes on the classical vocabulary, and still earns its place in normal programmes through sheer quality.

When it was revived in 1968 the only survivor of the first cast was Fonteyn, as luminous as ever at the centre of the festivities. This time Nureyev was her partner, and for him Ashton arranged an extra solo – a set of fiendishly difficult and tricky steps designed to exploit his footwork and turns.

The result was not altogether happy – Nureyev seemed too strong for the light, airy filigree – but the pas de deux gained extra authority from the partnership. *The Times*, noting that the balance had been changed through 'the English quietness of one partner and the Russian enthusiasm of the other' thought the pas de deux had taken on 'a new, more volatile, more impassioned emphasis'. 'The piece is a delight,' wrote the *Financial Times*. 'Fonteyn brought tremendous artistry to her variation and to the tender pas de deux.' *The Guardian* thought that 'its brisk Ashtonian intricacy was more suited to the school of Talgarth Road than of the Kirov. Nonetheless Nureyev carried it off with his undeniable star quality.' *The Sun* was carried away. 'Looking at Fonteyn and Nureyev in this gorgeous *Birthday Offering* . . . the astounding feature about these two is the electricity between them', and the *Sunday Telegraph* dared to suggest that the ballet was 'a great deal better than ever before.'

Not everybody was convinced; the *Daily Telegraph* thought that 'Dame Margot Fonteyn . . . danced the central role a shade less brilliantly than on former occasions while her partner over-stressed what should have been some of his smoothest dancing feats'. *The Observer* considered that 'most of the joy, wit and elegance had faded', while the *Sunday Times* noticed that 'Fonteyn at the end . . . does not disdain to play up the super-schmalz, flicking up her eyes and baring her teeth as the last note is coaxed, like a parting kiss, from the orchestra.'

But a few nights later the *Westminster News* was recording: 'The biggest uproar in the opera house for some time. The ovation . . . after *Birthday Offering* lasted throughout the extended interval and into the overture of *Jazz Calendar* and was only then quelled by some angry (and quite rightly) member of the audience.'

Pelléas et Mélisande

First performance together London, 26 March, 1969
Choreography Roland Petit **Music** Arnold Schoenberg
Design Jacques Dupont

THE MODIFIED success of Roland Petit's *Paradise Lost* was perhaps the basis for hopes that another work by the same choreographer could turn out a full-sized triumph for another gala. The story of *Pelléas et Mélisande* was pared down to a simple triangular love story between the heroine, the hero and his jealous brother. The music chosen was Arnold Schoenberg's early symphonic poem around Maeterlinck's drama, a rather turgid score lasting over forty minutes – too long by half, as it turned out. Petit reverted to acrobatic romantics, with elaborate lifts and aerial manoeuvres for Fonteyn and a series of yearning and anguished movements for Nureyev, including a death-agony solo which lasted minutes beyond any believability. The best element in the ballet was Dupont's filmy setting, with a huge dappled gauze which rose at the start to form a tent of foliage and descended later to represent the streaming tresses of Mélisande's hair.

Widespread sympathy could be felt for the stars at finding themselves in such a feeble production and both received some tributes. 'Fonteyn survives her role with magnificent equanimity, even preserving a calm dignity while being dragged all over the stage on her bottom,' wrote *The Times*. 'Right from Rudolf Nureyev's first entrance . . . it was his personality that dominated Roland Petit's new ballet,' recorded the *Evening News*. But the ballet itself was universally condemned. *The Observer* described it as 'A work of resounding mediocrity . . . which wallows in extravagance and stagy emotionalism.' The *Daily Telegraph* was 'disappointed' and *Dance and Dancers* found it 'nothing less than a disaster'.

The Financial Times thought that 'Fonteyn strives with all her immense gifts to convince us that Mélisande is a real and tragic figure. Nureyev dances with unflagging virtuosity'; but the *Daily Express* found it simply 'the most purposeless and least original concoction ever created for these stars to dance.' 'Now it has gone to America and I hope it never comes back,' wrote the *Dancing Times*. It never did.

Mira

Apparitions

First performance together London, 24 July, 1970
Choreography Frederick Ashton **Music** Franz Liszt
Design Cecil Beaton

THE GALA to salute the retirement of Sir Frederick Ashton after twenty-five years with the Royal Ballet was organized with skill by Sir Robert Helpmann to illustrate the many phases of Ashton's career. Fonteyn and Nureyev appeared together in two works – the recent *Marguerite and Armand* and a historical revival, *Apparitions*.

Written in 1936, *Apparitions* was originally an extended exercise in Ashton's dramatic romantic style, an adaptation by Constant Lambert of the story of Berlioz's *Symphonie Fantastique*, in which a suicidal poet dreams of his beloved as the poison takes effect. The excerpt for the gala was one of the interludes of pure dance, a swirling pas de six in which heroine and poet waltz and flirt in dream-like ecstasy.

'The air was charged with nostalgia' recorded *The Stage*. 'Fonteyn came back to wear Cecil Beaton's alluring black ball dress . . . It was indeed wonderful to see her not only dancing again . . . but looking just as right for the young girl.' Nureyev's modest incursion into this home-grown work went virtually un-recorded, apart from a report of an overheard aside from Robert Helpmann, the original hero. 'My interpretation was quite different,' he muttered ironically as the Russian leapt and spun.

G B L Wilson

G B L Wilson

Don Juan

First performance together London, 4 March, 1975
Choreography John Neumeier **Music** Christoph Gluck
Design Filippo Sanjust

A S AN OFFERING at a 1975 royal gala, Nureyev suggested that Fonteyn join him in a ballet he had recently danced in in Canada, *Don Juan*. Although the full work is decidedly complicated, the roles of the hero and the White Lady who haunts him all his life are clean cut and contain some lyrical pas de deux. John Neumeier made for them an extended extract from his ballet which included dances out of several different episodes.

The effectiveness of the extract was in doubt ('this arbitrary and rather thin fragment', the *Financial Times* called it), but the stars, especially Fonteyn, aroused enthusiasm. 'Margot Fonteyn could hardly fail to provide the highlight of any performance in which she appears,' wrote *The Times*, 'And this time she had a marvellous new role to dance . . . The many unusual lifts of the duets suit her long, flexible line beautifully and nobody could convey better the idea of the one unobtainable love who proves finally to be the angel of death . . .' The same critic found Nureyev's interpretation ideal. 'The character's blend of stellar magnetism, insolent charm and sexual voracity seems custom-built for him,' wrote *The Observer*, which had described Fonteyn as 'shedding a soft illumination over her lover'. 'She looks as fragile and as lyrical as ever,' recorded the *Daily Mail*, while the *Evening News* noted that 'somehow she makes all the other stars look dim.'

'The ethereal ghost of divine Donna Margot came to fetch Don Rudolf away,' wrote *The Sunday Times*. 'And serve him right with his proud Velasquez strut and his naughty irresistible mannerism of flicking away an unruly lock of hair. Fonteyn's ovation continued for fifteen minutes, during all of which time it rained daffodils.'

Linda Vartoogian

Anthony Crickmay

Lucifer

First performance together New York, 19 June, 1975
Choreography Martha Graham **Music** Halim El-Dabh
Design Leonardo Locsin

THE GREAT debate in the dance world during the middle of the twentieth century concerned the rival claims of classical ballet and what came to be known as 'modern dance'. The new idiom was mainly the child of the American dancer and choreographer Martha Graham and started as a reaction against the triviality of much academic ballet. Compromise seemed unthinkable, but time did its work and the final truce between the two styles was symbolically signed one evening in New York when the two celebrated classical dancers appeared in a short ballet specially composed for them by the eighty-one-year-old rebel for a gala in aid of her school. 'Not since the lion and the lamb did their fabled bedtime act has there been such an unlikely but happy merging of differences,' wrote the *New York Times*.

Lucifer was primarily a vehicle for Nureyev, who had been the first classical star to cross the divide into the territory of modern dance; he had appeared in ballets by uncompromisingly modern choreographers such as Tetley, Béjart, Murray Louis and Paul Taylor and the progression to Martha Graham's style of dance was already half accomplished. For Fonteyn, who even in Petit's non-classical ballets had danced on point, the change was more drastic; but once again her spirit of adventure and curiosity led her on.

Unfortunately, Fonteyn had only a few days to learn the role of Night and she danced a somewhat modified version of it. Nureyev had longer to learn and practised assiduously. 'I started him on the floor as I teach any beginner,' said Graham. 'He has to do it over and over again as he learns. He does not intellectualize. He repeats until it speaks back to him through the body, through the bloodstream.'

The subject seems also to have come to birth gradually. 'I felt it should be something created round him, he was at that time in his life when he needed that kind of centring. Then I thought of the thing he is and I started with the idea "Tyger, tyger burning bright, in the forests of the night". And then I thought of the idea of Lucifer.' He was not, to her mind, a Satanic but a Promethean figure, a bringer of fire and light who, when he fell, became half-man. 'I felt that curious explosive self-mockery, that lament for the peace of nothingness, was part of Lucifer and part of my life and Rudolf's life.'

Writing from New York, a correspondent in *Dance and Dancers* found that the splendour of the occasion and the designs almost overwhelmed the ballet. But she recorded that Graham had created 'a splendiferous role for Nureyev . . . From the moment we see him lying sprawled on the rock dressed only in a brief girdle, we sense his vulnerability and half-human, half-god-like existence. Nureyev, his right leg heavily bandaged from a sprain, danced the role with the feline grace of a leopard. His Grahamesque movements such as the 'bison' jump and contractions seemed a little forced, but essentially the role was danced with understanding . . . Although her movements were not Graham-style, Fonteyn brought her magnificent performing ability and stage presence to the work. Although dancing in bare feet must have been strange to her, she enacted the role seductively. Her aplomb seemed unshakeable.'

Foreseeably, Nureyev made more impact in the modern idiom than Fonteyn. 'This sort of thing is not for her,' concluded the *Daily News*, which thought that Nureyev, on the other had 'adapted to modern dance technique with surety and power'. The *New York Times* wrote 'He not only manages the duality of the character with exceptional subtlety, he also dances the choreography with a natural authority . . . He moves with a pantherine Grahamesque grace, he uses her cloaks and trains with imperious distinction, and seems only to find a certain difficulty in some of the falls. Dame Margot looked oriental and gorgeous but her dancing did not have quite the right weight and density.'

When the ballet reached Washington, reactions were much the same. 'Although she looked ill at ease in the floor work, she was impressive as the imperious queen of the underworld,' wrote the *Washington Post* of Fonteyn. 'Nureyev was a different matter, he has been studying modern movements seriously.' The *New York Times*, discussing the difference between the classical and modern styles, quoted a saying of Graham: 'There are only two sorts of dancing – good and bad.' This, it concluded, was good.

Martha Swope

Martha Swope

The Moor's Pavane

First performance together Washington, 8 July, 1975
Choreography José Limon **Music** Henry Purcell
Design Pauline Lawrence

SUBTITLED *Variations on a Theme of Othello*, this pas de quatre by the Mexican-born choreographer, José Limon, ingeniously distils Shakespeare's study of the lethal workings of obsessional jealousy into a short, tense, court dance in which the partners alternate and salute and challenge each other in a deadly quadrille. Originally written in 1949, it quickly passed into the repertoire of several American companies. Shortly before his death, in the autumn of 1972, Limon mounted it for the Canadian National Ballet.

Nureyev was the Moor on this occasion and he included the work several times subsequently in the selection of short ballets he presented in his 'Nureyev and Friends' seasons. It was in one of these programmes that Fonteyn appeared with him in the ballet, as Desdemona. Nureyev was by now well known in the dominating part of Othello. From the first he had rejected any attempt to simulate an Arab or Negro appearance and relied on a darkish make-up which still allowed him to use his face to express emotion. 'He portrays this Othello with a furious desperation that is enormously effective,' the *New York Times* had written after his first appearance in the role in New York. 'His body is all tension – it looks appropriately ready for the psychiatrist's couch – and yet it is also beautiful in its confirmation of the Purcell music.'

Three years later the same newspaper commented on Fonteyn's performance. 'The idea of Dame Margot as Desdemona . . . was to say the least, titillating. Dame Margot's cool and wronged Desdemona was intelligently acted and done. It certainly had a Shakespearean feel for the role to it, but she danced the ballet with a confidence that quite belied the lack of modern-dance background.' *The Observer* wrote of her as 'exquisite as ever, opposite the potent Othello of Nureyev'.

The *Washington Post* however, was decidedly cryptic. 'It was a performance', it wrote, 'signifying that a great work of art is always greater than the sum of its participants, and this in turn was a reflection on their integrity as artists,' – a judgement which can be read in many ways. Fonteyn never returned to the role.

With Karen Kain as Emilia
and Paolo Bortoluzzi as Iago

Beverley Gallegos

Susan Cook

Amazon Forest

First performance together New York, 18 November, 1975
Choreography Frederick Ashton **Music** Heitor Villa-Lobos
Design José Varona

IT WAS doubtless as a compliment to his hosts that Ashton chose a piece of music (originally the accompaniment to a film) by the much-loved Brazilian composer Villa-Lobos for a pas de deux for Fonteyn, partnered by the Royal Ballet dancer David Wall, for a gala in Rio de Janeiro in August 1975. To a mellifluous score he set a series of fluid movements in a mood vaguely ranging from yearning to ecstasy. It did not demand very much of either dancer, but exploited Fonteyn's lyrical style.

When Fonteyn joined Nureyev for one of his 'Nureyev and Friends' seasons in New York three months later, the work was included in the mixed programme. The *Daily News* found it 'a frustrating snippet', but the *New York Times* praised Fonteyn's 'iridescent and delightful performance in a light and slight love pas de deux. This was brief, rhapsodic and had Dame Margot whirled across the stage by Mr Nureyev, with serpentine and sinuous arms and her great liquid eyes all recalling . . . her sea sprite of fire and water in the same choreographer's *Ondine*. Mr Nureyev made a night of it. He partnered Dame Margot, particularly in the wistful magic of the closing Ashton duet to Villa-Lobos, with consistent gallantry and deference, always making himself, except of course in the solo dancing, subservient to his ballerina.'

Mira

Hamlet Prelude

First performance together London, 30 May, 1977
Choreography Frederick Ashton **Music** Franz Liszt
Design Carl Toms

FOR THE celebration of the Jubilee of Queen Elizabeth II, Ashton agreed to compose a short pas de deux for Fonteyn and Nureyev. He chose characters who were manifestly linked to those of the dancers – Ophelia with her tragic tenderness and Hamlet, a mixture of irony and passion. Finding a suitable musical framework in a short piece by Liszt – his 'Hamlet' symphonic study – he devised a short ballet around the melancholy relationship of the two Shakespearean lovers.

It was a relatively simple, flowing dance and made, perhaps, less impression than it might have done if there had been more time to prepare it. By ill chance Nureyev was involved in composing, producing and dancing in his own *Romeo and Juliet* at the time and had to leave his dress-rehearsal in order to appear.

However, it was, on the whole, well received. The *Daily Telegraph* thought the work easily the most exciting of the new ballets and that Fonteyn's Ophelia recalled her interpretation of the same character in Helpmann's *Hamlet*. But 'Ashton gave her far more varied and sensitive choreography. She made the most of it, dancing with exquisite grace and pathos, shading finally into madness. As Hamlet, Nureyev was at his most romantic, but suddenly became stern and brutal, a prey to his own inner conflicts.' *The Observer* described the ballet as 'an elusive encounter in which Ophelia fluttered like a diaphanous moth round the flickering figure, half-mocking, half-infatuated, of the Prince.'

There were reservations, especially about the limitations of Fonteyn's role. *The Guardian* ventured only that the work 'provided an appropriate touch of nostalgia'. But the *Daily Mail* was confident about the conjunction of three such major talents. It guessed that 'the combined genius of Fonteyn, Nureyev and Ashton may just have provided us with a ballet that will survive long enough to make this gala a truly memorable one.'

Leslie Spatt

L'Après-midi d'un Faune

First performance together London, 21 June, 1979
Choreography Vaslav Nijinsky **Music** Claude Debussy
Design Léon Bakst

This ballet, which Nijinsky wrote for himself, makes no technical demands; the mood is evoked through physical presence. When Nureyev and Fonteyn danced it together their performance was hailed by most of the critics as a triumph. Nureyev 'held the audience in thrall', wrote *The Guardian*, and the *Sunday Telegraph* declared that 'their partnership still has its particular magic'.

Le Spectre de la Rose

First performance together London, 23 June, 1979
Choreography Mikhail Fokine **Music** Carl-Maria von Weber
Design Léon Bakst (Nureyev's costume Toer van Schayk)

Nureyev introduced this Nijinsky role into his 1979 London season and Fonteyn suddenly decided to dance the part she had learnt direct from Nijinsky's partner, Karsavina. Few critics were at the unannounced event, but *The Observer* wrote 'The tenderness between the two artists was never more evident'.